DORLING KINDERSLEY **DK** EYEWITNESS BOOKS

SHAKESPEARE

Boy player

Hornbook

Quill pens

Horn inkwells

Nine men's morris game

Hautboy, or shawm

Model of the Globe theater

Spanish galleon

Hare

Skull used as a prop

Schoolboy

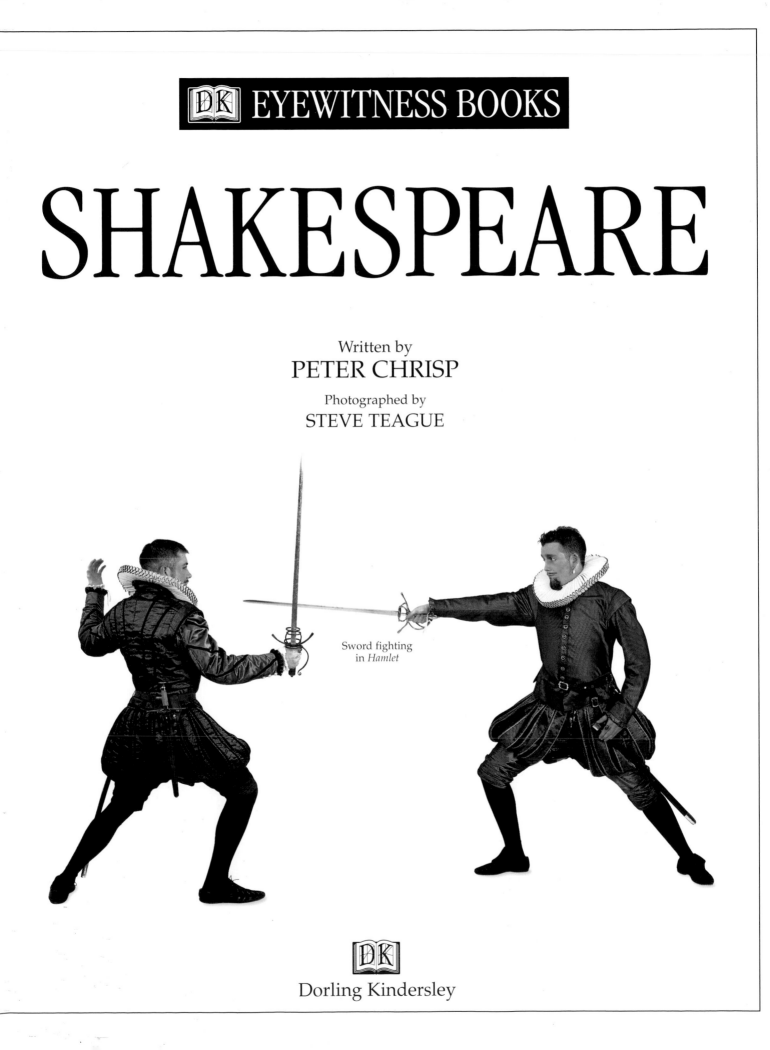

DK EYEWITNESS BOOKS

SHAKESPEARE

Written by
PETER CHRISP

Photographed by
STEVE TEAGUE

Sword fighting
in *Hamlet*

DK

Dorling Kindersley

Black rat

LONDON, NEW YORK, MUNICH, PARIS,
MELBOURNE, DELHI

Sword and
dagger

Crown
used as
a prop

Project editor Louise Pritchard
Art editor Jill Plank
Editor Annabel Blackledge
Assistant art editors Kate Adams, Yolanda Carter
Senior editor Monica Byles
Senior art editors Jane Tetzlaff, Clare Shedden
Category publisher Jayne Parsons
Senior managing art editor Jacquie Gulliver
Senior production controller Kate Oliver
Picture researcher Franziska Marking
Picture librarians Sally Hamilton, Rachel Hilford
DTP designer Matthew Ibbotson, Justine Eaton
Jacket designer Dean Price
US editors Margaret Parrish, Gary Werner

This Eyewitness ® Guide has been conceived by
Dorling Kindersley Limited and Editions Gallimard

First American Edition, 2002
02 03 04 05 10 9 8 7 6 5 4 3 2 1

Published in the United States by
DK Publishing, Inc.
95 Madison Avenue
New York, New York 10016

Bunch of
garden herbs

Rooster used
in cockfights

DK Publishing offers special discounts for bulk purchases for sales promotions
or premiums. Specific, large-quantity needs can be met with special editions,
including personalized covers, excerpts of existing guides, and corporate
imprints. For more information, contact Special Markets Department,
DK Publishing Inc., 95 Madison Avenue, New York, NY 10016, Fax 800-600-9098.

A Cataloging-in-Publication record
is available from the Library of Congress
ISBN 0-7894-8336-X (hc)
ISBN 0-7894-8337-8 (pb)

Color reproduction by
Colourscan, Singapore
Printed in China
by Toppan Printing Co.,
(Shenzhen Ltd.)

Bottom from
*A Midsummer
Night's Dream*

Traveling
library

See our complete
catalog at
www.dk.com

Elizabethan
noblewoman

Contents

Lute

Shakespeare's birthplace

WILLIAM SHAKESPEARE was born in 1564, in the small town of Stratford-upon-Avon, England. At that time, Stratford had only eight or nine streets and fewer than 1,500 inhabitants. It was a market town, where the local farmers could bring their crops, animals, and other goods to sell. William's exact birth date is not known, but it would have been shortly before his christening, which took place on April 26. He was born into a prosperous middle-class family. His father, John, was one of Stratford's leading men and served on the council that governed the town. He made his living as a glove-maker, and also dealt in wool and timber.

A BARD IS BORN
William was born in this house on Henley Street, Stratford. The house has now been turned into the Birthplace Museum. The rooms have been furnished to show how they would have looked in Shakespeare's time.

16th-century civic maces

Maces were originally used as weapons

Blue dye came from the woad plant

Yellow dye came from the weld plant, or "dyer's broom"

Red dye came from madder roots

POSITION OF AUTHORITY
In 1568, John Shakespeare was elected high bailiff of Stratford, which was like being a mayor. His authority was symbolized by an ornamental staff called a mace. This was carried before him in processions by an officer called a sergeant at mace.

LEFTOVERS FOR SALE
Wool was a by-product of glove making. John Shakespeare bought sheepskins from the butchers. He cut away the wool and prepared the skins so that he could use them for his gloves. He then sold the wool to Stratford's dyers and weavers. It was dyed using a variety of local plants and woven into cloth.

16th-century velvet and satin mittens embroidered with flowers

GLOVE STORY
In the 16th century, wealthy people wore fashionable, beautifully embroidered gloves like these mittens. People also wore gloves for warmth and protection. John Shakespeare may have sold embroidered gloves, but would not have made them himself. Embroidery was done mainly at home by women.

WORK FROM HOME
John Shakespeare's workshop was situated in the house on Henley Street. He prepared the animal skins, then cut and sewed them into gloves. John probably also sold his gloves, wallets, and other leather goods from his workshop.

Walls were covered with decorative tapestries or cheaper painted cloth

Straw was used as a mattress

CROWDED HOUSE
William grew up in a crowded house, and probably shared a space-saving "trundle bed" like this with some of his brothers and sisters. In the daytime, the lower bed could be wheeled right under the upper one. In Shakespeare's day, it was normal for children to keep warm by sharing the same bed.

MOTHER'S ROOM
This is thought to be the room where John's wife Mary gave birth to William and his seven brothers and sisters. It has been furnished to show how it may have looked after the birth of William's brother Richard in 1574. A cradle stands by the bed, and the basket is full of strips of linen called swaddling bands used to wrap babies.

Knobs and grooves carved by hand on a lathe

BUILT TO IMPRESS
As a small child, William probably sat in a high chair just like this. The elaborate decoration would have made it an expensive item of furniture. The carving was not for the baby's benefit, but to impress neighbors and visitors. Parents who could afford such a fancy high chair would have given an impression of wealth and good taste.

FAMILY MISFORTUNES
For a time, John Shakespeare's businesses were very successful, and he could afford expensive tableware, like these pewter dishes in the hall of the Birthplace Museum. In 1576, however, John's businesses began to fail. He got into debt and lost his position of importance in the town. William, who was 12 years old at the time, must have been affected by his father's money problems. When he grew up, he would work to restore his family's fortunes.

Going to school

AT ABOUT THE AGE of four, William Shakespeare would have gone to a "petty school" to learn to read. This was a small private school for boys and girls. At six, girls left the petty school to be taught at home by their mothers or, if they were rich, by private tutors. At the same age, if their parents could afford not to send them out to work, sons of middle-class men like John Shakespeare were provided with free education at the local grammar school. The purpose of the school was to teach Latin. At the time, people needed to know Latin if they wanted to go to a university, in order to follow a career in politics, law, medicine, teaching, or the Clergy.

BIRCH BEATING
Schoolmasters always carried a bundle of birch twigs. This was used to beat pupils when they were disobedient or when they made mistakes with their schoolwork.

"Our Father which art in Heaven" in Latin, from the Lord's Prayer

READING MATTERS
Children learned to read using a "hornbook," a piece of wood covered with printed paper, protected by a sheet of transparent horn. This hornbook is for learning the Lord's Prayer in Latin. Every pupil had to learn this prayer by heart.

RELUCTANT PUPILS
Most boys hated going to school. The hours were long, the lessons were dull, and their behavior was strictly controlled. "When I should have been at school," wrote author Thomas Nashe in 1592, "I was close under a hedge or under a barn playing at Jack-in-the-box."

19th-century painting illustrating Jaques's speech about a whining schoolboy in *As You Like It*

With his hornbook and satchel, the boy described in As You Like It *sets off "unwillingly to school."*

Feathers tended to get in the way, but were sometimes left on for show.

The pen had to be dipped into the ink at regular intervals.

A selection of goose feather quills

"And then the whining schoolboy, with his satchel, and shining morning face, creeping like a snail unwillingly to school."

WILLIAM SHAKESPEARE
Jaques in *As You Like It*

PEN AND INK
Before children could begin learning to write, they had to make themselves a pen called a quill from a goose feather. They trimmed the feather to the right shape and size using a "penknife," then cut the tip at an angle to make a point. Ink was kept in a pot called an inkwell, made of sheep's horn, wood, pottery, or metal.

Horn inkwells

BALANCING ACT
There were no desks in Tudor schools, so pupils had to rest their work on their knees. This was no problem when they were reading from textbooks and hornbooks, but it must have made things very difficult when they had to practice their handwriting! In the petty school, children sat on stools, but older schoolboys sat on long benches called forms.

As he reads, the schoolboy follows the words with his finger.

TRAGIC INSPIRATION
At school, Shakespeare was introduced to the work of ancient Roman authors such as Seneca (4 BC–65 AD). Seneca wrote serious plays called tragedies, which dealt with the suffering and death of great heroes. When Shakespeare grew up to be a writer, one of his first plays was a bloodthirsty tragedy inspired by Seneca called *Titus Andronicus*.

OLD FAVORITE
Shakespeare's favorite writer was the poet Ovid (43 BC–17 AD), whose poem *Metamorphoses* is a collection of stories drawn from ancient Greek and Roman myths. In 1598, a writer called Francis Meres compared Shakespeare to Ovid: "The sweet witty soul of Ovid lives in mellifluous and honey-tongued Shakespeare."

Religious conflict

THE 16TH CENTURY was a time of bitter religious divisions. All English people were Christian, but there were two rival versions of the faith: Catholicism and Protestantism. In 1534, Henry VIII broke with the Catholic Church and declared himself head of an Anglican, or English, Church. Under his son Edward VI (1547–53), the Anglican Church became Protestant. There was a swing back to Catholicism under Mary (1553–58), but Elizabeth (1588–1603) restored Protestantism, fining anyone who refused to worship in an Anglican church. The Protestants were split into Anglicans and Puritans, people who thought the break with Catholics had not gone far enough.

Mary, crowned Queen of Heaven, holds the baby Jesus

AN ENGLISH BIBLE
The Bible that Shakespeare knew is known as the Geneva Bible. Catholics used a Latin Bible, but Protestants thought that everyone should be able to read the book in their own language. When Mary came to the throne, a group of Protestants fled to Geneva, where they wrote this English translation.

QUEEN OF HEAVEN
Catholics prayed in front of statues of saints, such as Mary the mother of Christ, whom they called the Queen of Heaven. Protestants said that there were no special saints in heaven, and they condemned religious statues as idols. Under the Protestant king, Edward VI, statues like this one were smashed to pieces all over England.

COUNTING PRAYERS
Rosary beads were used by Catholics to keep count of prayers. Catholics believed that the repetition of certain Latin prayers, such as Ave Maria, or Hail Mary, would help them to get to heaven. Protestants said that this was superstition.

Leather carrying case

Chalice for giving wine at communion

Plate for communion wafers

Christ depicted on the cross

BODY AND BLOOD
Catholics believed that their priests had the power to turn bread and wine into the body and blood of Christ. Priests carried portable communion sets like this to perform the ceremony for Catholics worshipping in secret. Anglican priests performed a similar ceremony, but they did not believe that the bread and wine were really changed into Christ's body and blood.

Bottle for carrying wine

BLOODY MARY

Queen Mary had almost 290 Protestants burned at the stake, and fellow Protestants celebrated them as martyrs – heroes who died for their faith. The queen was nicknamed "Bloody Mary." Elizabeth had 193 Catholics executed. They were killed not for their beliefs, but for treason, since they were loyal to a foreign ruler – the Pope.

At each end of the cross are portraits of Matthew, Mark, Luke, and John, authors of the Christian Gospels

A Puritan father gives his family religious instruction

PURITAN BELIEFS

Puritans wanted to strip away all the features of Christian worship that did not appear in the Bible. They thought that the Anglican Church should get rid of bishops, vestments, or church clothes, and all elaborate ceremonies, which they called "popish practices." Many Puritans rejected the use of the crucifix, or cross, as a Christian symbol. They looked with horror on richly jeweled crosses.

Simple crucifix

The lamb, a sacrificial animal, stands for Christ, whom Christians believe sacrificed himself to save humanity

Richly decorated Catholic crucifix

PLOTS AGAINST THE QUEEN

In 1587, Queen Elizabeth had her cousin, Mary Stuart, Queen of Scots, executed. Mary, a Catholic, had been a prisoner in England since 1568, when she fled from Scotland after being defeated in battle by the Scottish Protestants. She was beheaded after becoming the focus of a series of plots by English Catholics. They had planned to murder Elizabeth and replace her with Mary. Such plots were encouraged by the Pope, the head of the Catholic Church, who had declared in 1570 that Elizabeth was no longer the rightful queen.

MIXED BELIEFS

Catholics and Anglicans both used the cross on which Christ died as a symbol of their faith, although Catholic crosses were more highly decorated. It is hard to tell what Shakespeare would have thought of this cross. In the late 17th century, a writer called Richard Davies said that Shakespeare "died a Papist" (Catholic). His plays do show certain Catholic features, such as characters that swear by saints. However, one play, *King John*, is strongly anti-Catholic. We don't know what Shakespeare really believed. Perhaps, like many English people, he had a mixture of beliefs.

A country childhood

FIELDS OF FRANCE
When Shakespeare was growing up, he would often have seen oxen pulling plows in the fields around Stratford. In *Henry V*, he compares France to an unplowed field overgrown with weeds, with a plow rusting away.

WILLIAM SHAKESPEARE grew up in the heart of the countryside. He knew the farmers' fields around Stratford, the meadows where wildflowers grew, and the Forest of Arden to the north. As an adult writing plays in London, Shakespeare drew on his memories of the countryside. His plays are full of accurate descriptions of flowers, trees, wild birds and animals, clouds, and the changing seasons. In *Macbeth*, Shakespeare describes night falling with the words, "Light thickens, and the crow makes wing to the rooky wood," and in *Romeo and Juliet*, Capulet, hearing of his daughter's death, says, "Death lies on her like an untimely frost upon the sweetest flower in all the field."

LITTLE LIVESTOCK
Farm animals were smaller in Shakespeare's time than they are now. Some of today's rare breeds give us an idea of what they looked like. The Bagot goat has not changed since 1380, when King Richard II gave a herd to Sir John Bagot.

Longhorn

Livestock

In the 1500s, farm animals had many uses. Cattle were milked and used to pull plows. Sheep provided wool, meat, and milk. Goats were used for milk, meat, horn, and leather. In November, when most livestock was killed because animal feed was in short supply, pigs were fed on acorns in the woods, to provide a valuable source of fresh meat for the end of the winter.

"When icicles hang by the wall, And Dick the shepherd blows his nail, And Tom bears logs into the hall, And milk comes frozen home in pail ..."

WILLIAM SHAKESPEARE
Winter in *Love's Labours Lost*

Bagot goat

Wheat

Pitchfork, for moving piles of hay, straw, and harvested cereal

Oats   Rye   Barley

Crook, to hold stalks together when harvesting with a sickle

Sickle, used to cut crops

DAILY BREAD
Farmers grew various cereals, which were used to make bread. Expensive bread was made from wheat, while cheaper bread was made from barley and rye. If crops failed, people had to eat bread made from oats or even acorns.

HARVEST TIME
Simple tools, including crooks and sickles, were used to harvest crops. The harvested cereal was loaded onto a wagon with a pitchfork and taken away to be threshed, or beaten, to separate the edible grains from the chaff, or stalks.

Crops and flowers
Country life in Shakespeare's day was a never-ending cycle of plowing, sowing, and harvesting. The work was long and hard, and people's lives depended on the success of the crops. Nothing of what the countryside had to offer was wasted. Even wildflowers and plants were harvested for use in cooking, medicine, and the home. Shakespeare used images of crops, plants, and wildflowers to bring his writing to life.

Peasant's cart

Cowslip

Nettle

Bristles cover the whole body

POSIES AND POISONS
Shakespeare used his knowledge of wildflowers when writing many of his plays. In *Hamlet*, the mad Ophelia makes "fantastic garlands" of "crow flowers, nettles, daisies, and long purples." The wicked queen in *Cymbeline* sends her ladies to gather violets, cowslips, and primroses, in order to make poison.

Pig

Sweet violet

Primrose

Illustration of Ophelia from *Flowers in Shakespeare's Garden* by Walter Crane, 1906

13

Country fun

With its sharp tusks, the wild boar was a dangerous animal to hunt

IN THE COUNTRYSIDE around Shakespeare's home town of Stratford, people made their own entertainment when they had the opportunity. They kicked footballs made from inflated pigs' bladders, practiced archery, and played simple board games. The wild creatures from the surrounding fields and forests provided locals with sports, as well as meat for their tables. The poor hunted small birds and animals, while the wealthy preferred to chase larger prey such as wild boar and deer in the forests. Deer could also be found in Sir Thomas Lucy's private park at Charlecote, five miles (eight kilometers) east of Stratford.

DOST THOU LOVE HAWKING?
A lord in *The Taming of the Shrew* asks the question "Dost thou love hawking?" Shakespeare certainly did, and he mentions it more often in his plays than he does any other sport. When the heroine of *Romeo and Juliet* wants to call back her departing lover, she cries, "O! for a falconer's voice, to lure this tassel-gentle back again." A "tassel-gentle" was a name for a male peregrine falcon.

The hood stopped the bird from flying away

Gyrfalcon

Hunting

Hunting and falconry (hunting using birds of prey) were popular pastimes for rich and poor alike. Nobles kept peregrine falcons and gyrfalcons, which they used to catch herons, ducks, pigeons, and rooks. Poorer people kept goshawks, which were thought to be less noble birds. Goshawks were flown after hares, rabbits, and partridges.

Hare, used mainly for its meat

Slow, strong mastiff dog, used to kill wild boars

The falconer gripped the jesses, or leather straps, attached to the bird's legs

Bloodhound, used to sniff out wild boar and deer

HUNTING HOUNDS
There were various types of hunting dog, each one bred for a different purpose. Greyhounds were bred for speed. In *Henry VI Part Three*, Queen Margaret compares the enemies pursuing her to two greyhounds: "Edward and Richard, like a brace of greyhounds having the fearful fleeing hare in sight ... are at our backs."

Swift greyhound, used for coursing (running after hares)

Jingling bells allowed the falconer to find the bird when it went out of sight

A heavy glove protected the hand from the bird's sharp talons

Backgammon
game

RICH GAME, POOR GAME
Shakespeare mentions two board games in his plays: tables, or backgammon, which was played by the wealthy; and nine men's morris, which was played by the poor. Shepherds often cut the lines of the morris board in the ground and played with pebbles.

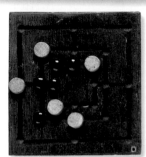

Nine men's
morris game

SUMMER CELEBRATIONS
On May 1, people celebrated the arrival of summer by dancing around poles that were decked with flowers and ribbons, called maypoles. Collecting blossoms to hang over doors, or "going-a-maying," was another Maytime custom. In *A Midsummer Night's Dream*, Shakespeare writes: "They rose early to observe the rite of May."

Gentlemen shoot
arrows at a target on
the village green

SPORTS ON SUNDAY
On Sundays, Englishmen practiced archery. The original reason was practical: the longbow was an important weapon in warfare and was also used in hunting. In war, the bow was being replaced by firearms, but archery remained a popular sport. The queen herself was a skilled archer.

Games and festivals

Although country people worked hard, at quiet times in the farming year they found time for games and sports, such as nine men's morris, football, cockfighting, and archery. There were also festivals throughout the year to celebrate the changing seasons, religious events, and other special occasions, such as royal visits.

ENTERTAINING ROYALTY
The most exciting event in the countryside was a visit from Queen Elizabeth. The local nobility spent vast sums of money on the entertainment, such as this water show, put on for her in 1591. Elizabeth spent much of her time traveling around England, and people in the countryside looked forward to seeing her.

TELLING TALES
According to one story, Shakespeare had to flee from Stratford after being caught poaching deer in Sir Thomas Lucy's deer park. This story comes from Shakespeare's first biography, written in 1709 by John Rowe. He based his book on tales Stratford people were telling about the playwright.

The lost years

Oil painting of a mother and child in christening dress, c. 1595

We know little of what Shakespeare did from the time he left school, at about the age of 15, until 1592, when he was described as an up-and coming playwright in London. This period is called Shakespeare's "lost years." Church records have revealed that, in November 1582, William Shakespeare married a local farmer's daughter called Anne Hathaway. He was 18, while Anne was 26 and expecting their first child, Susanna, who was born the following May. In 1585, twins arrived, who were named Judith and Hamnet. Many theories have been suggested as to what else may have happened during the lost years, most of which are based more on imagination than on fact.

A PLACE IN HEAVEN
One in three babies died in the 1500s. Because unchristened babies would not go to heaven, christenings were important, and parents dressed their babies in fine clothes for the event. Susanna Shakespeare was baptized in Stratford on May 26, 1583.

HATHAWAY'S HOUSE
William's wife Anne grew up in the little village of Shottery, a mile (2 km) to the west of Stratford. Today, the house where she lived is known as Anne Hathaway's Cottage. It is not really a cottage at all, but a large farmhouse with twelve rooms.

Hunting for clues

For hundreds of years, scholars have hunted for clues that might explain what Shakespeare was doing during his lost years. Some have searched through documents written in the 1580s, looking for Shakespeare's name. Others have tried to find the answers in his plays and poems. His writing shows knowledge of types of work including medicine, soldiering, and the law, which suggests that he may have had some personal experience of them.

Cloth shears

Sheep shears

Unprepared sheep's wool

FATHER'S FOOTSTEPS
In Shakespeare's time, it was common for at least one son to follow his father into the family business. William may well have spent time helping John Shakespeare in his wool dealing business. The playwright later became a shrewd businessman, possibly using skills that he learned buying and selling wool.

Wool is carded, or combed, in preparation for spinning

Ball of thread

Spindle, used to spin wool into a thread

Coneys,
or rabbits

Wood
pigeons

Goose

MILITARY INTELLIGENCE
In the 1800s, Shakespeare scholar W.J. Thoms argued that the playwright's military knowledge meant that he had served as a soldier. Thoms found a document naming a soldier called William Shakespeare. But this man was serving in 1605, when our Shakespeare was a famous and successful playwright.

MEDICINE MAN
Shakespeare's work shows that he had some knowledge of medicine, but his characters are often scornful of physicians, or doctors. Macbeth says, "Throw physic to the dogs," and Timon of Athens says, "Trust not the physician."

STAGING A SLAUGHTER
In 1693, John Dowdall, a visitor to Stratford, was told that Shakespeare had worked as a butcher. Soon after this, writer John Aubrey recorded the same story, adding that when William killed a calf, "He would do it in a high style, and make a speech."

Spike to make holes for stitching

Elizabethan trenchers, or plates, decorated with paintings and verses representing professions

Half-moon leather knife

Hooked leather knife

GREEN FINGERS
Shakespeare's characters often refer to flowers and plants, sowing, pruning, weeding, and other gardening activities. This could mean that he worked as a gardener for a time, or simply that he took an interest in his own garden.

CASE CLOSED
Shakespeare's plays are full of legal terms. In 1790, English scholar Edmund Malone suggested that the playwright gained this knowledge working in a legal office. In fact, Shakespeare was involved in several legal cases, which may explain his understanding of the law.

LEATHER WORKING
Shakespeare is likely to have learned leather-working skills in his father's glove making workshop. After leaving school, with his family facing hard times, William may well have helped his father, using tools like these to make gloves, belts, or shoes.

16th-century engraving of Richard Tarlton

TAKING TO THE STAGE
In the 1580s, several companies of actors visited Stratford, performing in the town's inn yards. England's leading company, the Queen's Men, performed in Stratford in 1587. Shakespeare would surely have seen the company, whose star was the clown Richard Tarlton. He even might have joined them. All we know for certain is that, at some point, William Shakespeare became a player, or actor.

Hand-colored engraving of players performing in an inn yard

Up to London

Apple seller

Iɴ ᴛʜᴇ 1580s, Shakespeare said goodbye to his family in Stratford and set off to seek his fortune in London. He was just one of thousands of country people who moved to the great city in the late 16th century. He found himself in a bustling, crowded place, with narrow, dark streets littered with all kinds of garbage. As a newcomer, Shakespeare would have been struck by the noise, the dirt, and the smells of the city. Crossing London Bridge, he might have been shocked by the sight of the heads of executed traitors rotting on poles. He would also have been impressed by the beauty of the grand churches and the riverside mansions of London's wealthy merchants and nobles.

A waterman was like a 16th-century taxi driver

Watermen worked either alone or in pairs

WESTWARD HO!
Walking near the Thames River, Shakespeare would have been greeted by the watermen's shouts of "Westward ho!" and "Eastward ho!" as they called for passengers. The watermen rowed Londoners up and down the river, and across to Bankside and back. The Thames was crowded with boats of all sizes, including the gilded royal barge taking Queen Elizabeth to and from her palace at Greenwich.

A view of London from the south, by Dutch artist Claes Jans Visscher, c. 1616

Every day, thousands of people were rowed across the river to the playhouses at Bankside

SPREADING CITY
When Shakespeare came to London, most people lived in the old part of the city on the north side of the Thames River, still surrounded by medieval walls. But London was spreading fast in all directions, swelled by the rising number of incomers. Bankside, on the south bank of the river, was rapidly becoming London's main entertainment center.

Merchant and
his wife, 1590

"Sack! Sack!
A sup of sack!"
shouts a man
selling wine

"Ink! Ink! Pen
and ink!" cries
a man selling
quills and ink

"Trinkets and
toys! Trinkets
and toys!" calls
the tinker

"Almanacs!"
cries a man
selling books
of predictions

"Mack-mack-
mackereel!"
shouts a
mackerel seller

SOUNDS OF THE CITY

London was full of street sellers shouting out
special cries to attract customers. Men and
women wandered the streets selling everything
from vegetables, fish, wine, toys, and books, to
quills and ink, fruit, brooms, pies, and second-
hand clothes. They competed for business with
the craftsmen and tradesmen working in the
shops that lined the noisy, narrow streets.

MERCHANTS' MIGHT

The city was run by wealthy businessmen called merchants.
The richest merchants served as officials, called aldermen,
on a ruling council headed by the Lord Mayor. Trade was
central to the prosperity of the city, and every craft and
trade had its own controlling organization called a guild.

BUILDING UP

Staple Inn, where wool was weighed
and taxed in Shakespeare's day, is one
of the few buildings still standing in
London that the playwright would
recognize. Land was expensive, so
people built upward. The top floors of
these towering buildings jutted outward
over the street, creating more space
inside, but blocking out light below.

*The Latin text along the top of the
map describes London as "The most
famous market in the entire world"*

*The bells of more than
100 churches rang out
across the city*

...POR...QUE TOTO ORBE CELEBERRIMUM

*Shakespeare worshipped
here, at St. Mary Overie's
Church, later known as
Southwark Cathedral*

*Traitors' heads were displayed on poles on London Bridge
to warn the public against committing treason*

MEASURE FOR MEASURE

The guilds controlled trade using standard weights. They
employed official measurers to check that members were
not cheating their customers. Anyone caught selling short
measures was locked in the stocks for punishment.

Set of 16th-century
standard weights

London shows

Having grown up in sleepy Stratford, William Shakespeare must have found London an exciting place to live. It was the largest city in northern Europe, and 10 times the size of any other English town. Even before the playhouses were built, London had many different entertainments to offer its citizens. Londoners enjoyed watching cruel bloodsports, such as fights between bulls, bears, and packs of dogs, and they often gathered to watch executions. Many people passed their time by gambling or playing sports, such as lawn bowling.

ENTERTAINMENT CENTER
This map of London dates from 1572, just before the first playhouses were built. At this time, the only buildings specifically intended for entertainment were cockfighting pits, and bull and bear baiting houses, such as the Bear Garden.

FIGHTING CHANCE
Setting a pair of roosters to fight each other was a popular 17th-century sport all over Britain. In London alone, there were several cockpits – small, round buildings – where a crowd could watch the birds fight to the death. Onlookers would bet on the outcome of these cockfights.

Rooster

Roosters fought with their beaks and spurred feet

Londoners gather to watch an execution

GORY GALLOWS
Londoners were used to the sight of blood, and watching executions for entertainment was a long-standing tradition. The executions of traitors were the most gruesome shows. The traitors were dragged to the gallows behind a horse. They were half-hanged, then brought down alive, so that their bellies could be cut open and their inner organs burned in front of them.

Gallows were often specially built for each execution

Wooden gallows

Site of the Swan (built between 1595 and 1596)

Modern bulldog

BORN TO BITE
At Bankside, Londoners could see bull baiting with bulldogs that had been specially bred and trained for the sport. The bulldogs, which were much larger than modern bulldogs, were trained to leap at the bull's face. They hung on to its nose or ears, while the angry bull did its best to shake it off.

IN IT FOR THE MONEY

Most of the early playhouses, including the Swan and the Rose, were built by businessmen. They saw them as a.way to make money. London's first playhouses were the Theatre, built in 1576, and the Curtain, built in 1577. Their round design was copied from earlier buildings like the Bear Garden.

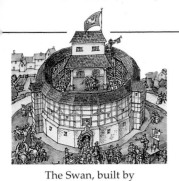

The Swan, built by
Philip Henslowe, dyer

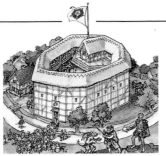

The Rose, built by Francis
Langley, goldsmith and draper

Site of the Theatre

Site of the Curtain

Bear Garden

Site of the Rose (built in 1587)

Bear baiting in the 16th century

STILLIARDS) Hansa, Gothica dictio, conuentum, vel congregationem sonans, multarum ciuitatum est confoederata Societas, tum ob praestita Societas, tum denique ad tranquillam Rerumpub. pacem, & ad modestam adolescentum institutionem conseruandam, instituta: plurimor. Regum, ac Principum, maxime Anglia, Gallia, Dania, ac Magna Moscouia, nec non Flandria, ac Brabantica Ducum priuilegiis, ac immunitatib. exornata fuit. Habet ea quatuor Emporia, (untores quidam vocant, in quibus ciuitatum negotiatores resident, suasque mercatus exercent Hor, alterum huic Londini, domestica oeconomia nitet, habens domum Gildehalla Teutonica quā vulgo Stilhard, nuncupat.

CONEYCATCHERS

Gambling was a risky pastime because London was full of criminals who made a living by cheating at cards and dice. These cheats were called coneycatchers, and they were always on the lookout for newcomers from the countryside like William Shakespeare. They called their victims coneys (rabbits).

A lucky gambler's winnings

The bears had their own names, such as Harry Hunks and Sackerson

Brown bear

TETHERED AND TOOTHLESS

In the Bear Garden, dogs were set against a bear tied to a stake. The bear's teeth were sometimes pulled out to give the dogs a better chance. Shakespeare's Scottish king Macbeth compares himself to a baited bear: "They have tied me to the stake; I cannot fly, but bearlike I must stay and fight the course."

Queen Elizabeth's court

WHEN THE QUEEN WAS NOT traveling the country, her court was based in the royal palaces around London, at Whitehall, Richmond, and Greenwich. Her royal barge carried her back and forth along the Thames River. Elizabeth surrounded herself with young male courtiers, who all competed for her favor. They flattered her by comparing her to the Roman moon goddess Diana, and called her "Gloriana," the glorious one. Londoners were fascinated by what Shakespeare called "court news"; in the play *King Lear*, "who loses and who wins, who's in, who's out."

PLAYERS AT COURT
Elizabeth enjoyed watching plays, although she never visited the public playhouses. Instead, the players were commanded to give private performances for the court in the palaces around London. Before he became a playwright, Shakespeare would have been known to the queen as a player, from court performances.

PELICAN QUEEN
In this 1574 portrait by Nicholas Hilliard, the 41-year-old queen wears a brooch showing a pelican. Female pelicans were wrongly thought to feed their young on their own blood. The queen wore this brooch to show that she cared for her people with the self-sacrificing love of a perfect mother.

White pearls symbolized the queen's purity

Pelican drawing blood from its breast

BEAUTY SECRETS
The ladies at court used all kinds of concoctions to make lotions and face washes, which they believed would remove pimples, freckles, and other "blemishes" of the skin. Herbs, spices, and wine were popular ingredients, but many of the recipes were harmful to health, and even poisonous.

Cloves

Ginger

Nutmeg

Bay

Spices and herbs were used in anti-freckle recipes

Opal

Belladonna drops from the deadly nightshade plant made the eyes sparkle

Mercury

Lemon

Lemon juice and poisonous mercury were used in face washes

17th-century traveling library

TRAVEL BOOKS
Elizabeth loved books and would have taken many with her when she traveled. Literature and poetry were also popular among her courtiers. Several of them, including Walter Ralegh, were talented poets. Ralegh wrote a long poem for Elizabeth called *The Ocean's Love for Cynthia*. Its title played on the queen's pet name for Ralegh, "Water." Cynthia was another name for the moon goddess.

Garnet fan-holder

Gold seal ring

Ruby

Garnet

Amethyst

Malachite

DRIPPING WITH JEWELS
Both men and women at court competed to look as expensively dressed as possible. Courtiers spent vast sums of money on jewels, which they used to decorate every item of clothing, from their shoes to their hats. Some of the jewels had special meanings. For example, gems shaped like a crescent moon were worn to show devotion to the queen as the moon goddess.

Signature of Elizabeth I

PRIDE COMES BEFORE A FALL
These are the signatures of the queen and her "favorite" of the 1590s, Robert Devereux, Earl of Essex (1566–1601). Essex was a proud man, who took the queen's favor for granted. In 1601, he led a rebellion that failed. Essex was beheaded. Shakespeare refers to him in *Much Ado About Nothing* in the lines "like favorites, made proud by princes, that advance their pride against the power that bred it."

Signature of Robert Devereux, Earl of Essex

ROYAL PROCESSION
Elizabeth was sometimes carried through London by her leading courtiers in a palanquin, or covered litter. The procession gave ordinary people the chance to catch a glimpse of their queen. This 19th-century woodcut was copied from a 1601 painting by Robert Peake. The queen was 68 when it was done, but the artist portrayed her as a young goddess surrounded by worshippers.

The playwrights

The Spanish Tragedy:
Or,
HIERONIMO is mad againe.

Containing the lamentable end of Don Horatio,
and Belimperia; With the pitifull Death
of HIERONIMO.

Newly Corrected, Amended, and Enlarged with new
Additions, as it hath of late beene divers
times Acted.

LONDON
Printed by Augustine Mathewes, for Francis Grove, and are to
bee sold at his Shoppe, neere the Sarrazens Head,
upon Snow-hill. 1633.

THE LONDON STAGE OF the early 1590s was dominated by the plays of a group of well-educated men nicknamed the "University Wits." The group included Robert Greene, Thomas Nashe, and Christopher Marlowe. They wrote plays in unrhymed lines of 10 syllables called "blank verse," like Marlowe's "Is this the face that launched a thousand ships?" By 1592, Shakespeare was also an established playwright. Greene wrote an attack on him that year, calling him an "upstart crow." He looked down on Shakespeare because he had not gone to a university. But Shakespeare was a success partly because he was a mere player – he knew what worked on stage and what did not.

SWEET REVENGE
Shakespeare learned to write by watching and acting in plays like Thomas Kyd's *The Spanish Tragedy*. Kyd (1558–1594) invented a new type of play called a "revenge tragedy," in which a murder is committed and then violently avenged. One of Shakespeare's first plays was the bloodthirsty revenge tragedy, *Titus Andronicus*.

The sloping surface allows the quill pen to be held at the right angle to the paper

SITTING COMFORTABLY
Before becoming a playwright, Thomas Kyd worked as a scrivener, or copier of documents. Sitting at a desk like this, he would have spent his days writing letters for people who could not write, and making neat copies of legal documents and plays. Most playwrights did not have special writing desks. They wrote wherever they could, often on tables in rented rooms and taverns.

Rusty nails

Oak leaf with gall

INKY INGREDIENTS
The black ink used by playwrights was made from a curious mixture of ingredients. The most important were swellings called galls found on oak trees. The galls were ground up and mixed with water or vinegar and a chemical called green vitriol, which was produced by pouring acid over rusty nails. The final ingredient was gum arabic, the dried sap of the acacia tree.

17th-century inkwell and quills

*"Now, Faustus, let thine eyes with horror stare
Into that vast perpetual torture-house,
There are the furies tossing damned souls
On burning forks. Their bodies broil in lead."*

CHRISTOPHER MARLOWE
Evil Angel in *Dr. Faustus*

TOOLS OF THE TRADE

All educated people knew how to cut a pen from a goose feather using a penknife. Playwrights and scriveners, who did a lot of writing, had to keep their penknife close at hand, ready for when the quill's tip wore out and a new one needed to be cut. Rich people used fancy knives with decorative carving, but playwrights like Shakespeare would probably have used plain, simple knives.

The word pen comes from the Latin word penna, *meaning feather*

LAST WORDS

Robert Greene (c. 1558–1592) was dying when he wrote his attack on Shakespeare. The document was found among his papers after his death and was published immediately. This picture of Greene writing in his funeral shroud symbolizes the fact that his words of attack came from beyond the grave.

William Shakespeare's signature

RAPID WRITING

Writing seemed to come easily to William Shakespeare. His fellow playwright Ben Jonson wrote that "Whatsoever he penned, he never blotted out a line." Jonson, a slow and careful writer, considered Shakespeare's ease and speed to be a sign of carelessness.

A Persian painting showing Timur on his throne

Carved penknives

Dr. Faustus summons a devil using magic

POETIC PLAYS

The writer who most influenced Shakespeare's poetry was Christopher Marlowe (1564–1593). Marlowe put stirring speeches into the mouths of tragic heroes such as Dr. Faustus, a scholar who sells his soul to the devil. Marlowe's influence can be seen in the opening line of Shakespeare's early play *Henry VI Part One*, "Hung be the heavens with black, yield day to night!"

ASTOUNDING TERMS

Marlowe's first play *Tamburlaine* tells the story of Timur, a 14th-century Turkish warrior. Marlowe portrays Tamburlaine (Timur), "Threatening the world with high astounding terms, and scourging kingdoms with his conquering sword."

England at war

ENGLAND'S ENEMY
Philip II of Spain ruled over a vast empire, with lands across Europe and in the Americas. He wanted to add England to his empire and bring the country back into the Catholic faith.

From 1585 to 1604, Protestant England was at war with Catholic Spain, ruled by King Philip II. The war created a mood of patriotism in the country, and people wanted to see plays drawn from English history with battles on the stage. So, in the 1590s, Shakespeare wrote nine plays dealing with English history, featuring kings, wars, and battles for the throne. A central theme of the plays is the need for order. At the time, people were worried about the war with Spain, the fact that their queen had no heir, the rumors of Catholic plots to dethrone her, and the risk of civil war.

Spanish galleons were taller than English ships and harder to maneuver

GOD'S WINDS
For England, a dangerous moment of the war with Spain came in 1588, when Phillip sent a huge war fleet called the Armada to invade. This ended in disaster for Spain. The Armada was beaten in battle and scattered by storms. English people took this as a sign that God was on their side.

Henry comes to parliament to make his claim to the throne

FAMOUS LAST WORDS
Shakespeare's play *Richard II* tells the story of the overthrow of King Richard II by his cousin Henry Bolingbroke, who became Henry IV. The play contains Shakespeare's most famous patriotic speech, spoken by the dying John of Gaunt: "This happy breed of men, this little world, this precious stone set in a silver sea ... this blessed plot, this earth, this realm, this England."

FAT FALSTAFF
Sir John Falstaff is the drunken old knight who befriends young Prince Hal in Shakespeare's two *Henry IV* plays. The plays show a series of rebellions against Henry IV, whose troubled reign is God's punishment for overthrowing Richard II. Prince Hal grows into a heroic figure who will make a great king, but first he must reject Falstaff.

FOR KING AND COUNTRY
Prince Hal reappears as the king in *Henry V*, the story of England's great victory over the French at the Battle of Agincourt in 1415. "Follow your spirit," cries the king, rallying his men, "and upon this charge, cry God for Harry, England, and Saint George!"

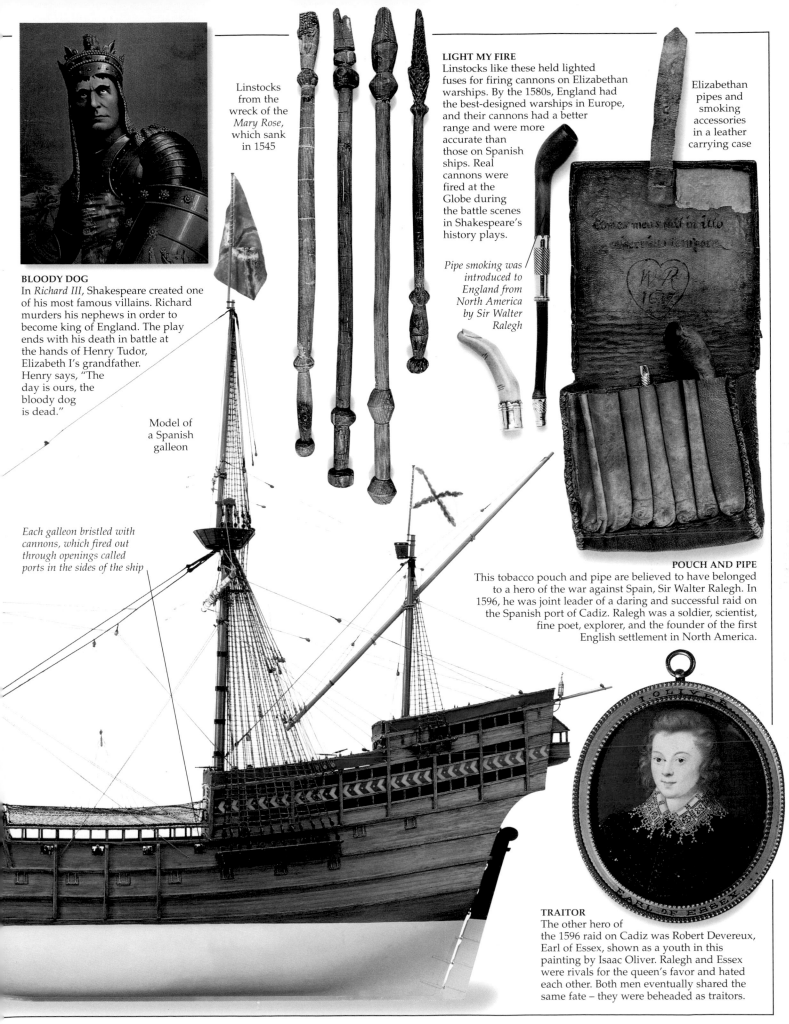

BLOODY DOG
In *Richard III*, Shakespeare created one of his most famous villains. Richard murders his nephews in order to become king of England. The play ends with his death in battle at the hands of Henry Tudor, Elizabeth I's grandfather. Henry says, "The day is ours, the bloody dog is dead."

Linstocks from the wreck of the *Mary Rose*, which sank in 1545

LIGHT MY FIRE
Linstocks like these held lighted fuses for firing cannons on Elizabethan warships. By the 1580s, England had the best-designed warships in Europe, and their cannons had a better range and were more accurate than those on Spanish ships. Real cannons were fired at the Globe during the battle scenes in Shakespeare's history plays.

Elizabethan pipes and smoking accessories in a leather carrying case

Pipe smoking was introduced to England from North America by Sir Walter Ralegh

Model of a Spanish galleon

Each galleon bristled with cannons, which fired out through openings called ports in the sides of the ship

POUCH AND PIPE
This tobacco pouch and pipe are believed to have belonged to a hero of the war against Spain, Sir Walter Ralegh. In 1596, he was joint leader of a daring and successful raid on the Spanish port of Cadiz. Ralegh was a soldier, scientist, fine poet, explorer, and the founder of the first English settlement in North America.

TRAITOR
The other hero of the 1596 raid on Cadiz was Robert Devereux, Earl of Essex, shown as a youth in this painting by Isaac Oliver. Ralegh and Essex were rivals for the queen's favor and hated each other. Both men eventually shared the same fate – they were beheaded as traitors.

Plague and poetry

DIRTY RATS
People did not know it, but the plague was carried by blood-sucking fleas that lived on the black rats that swarmed through the city's dirty streets. Between 1592 and 1593, plague-carrying fleas led to the deaths of almost 12,000 Londoners.

Black rat

Flea

OUTBREAKS OF A TERRIBLE disease called the plague were common in Elizabethan London. Nobody knew how the plague spread, but when there was an outbreak it seemed wise to avoid crowded places. By law, the city's playhouses could not open if more than 30 people had died in one week. Between 1592 and 1594, the plague was so bad that the playhouses had to stay closed for just over two years. The companies of actors left London to tour the countryside in order to make a living. There was no demand for Shakespeare to write new plays, so he turned to poetry.

"Rich men trust not in wealth,
Gold cannot buy you health:
Physic himself must fade.
All things to end are made,
The plague full swift goes by;
I am sick, I must die:
Lord have mercy on us."

THOMAS NASHE
Summer's Last Will and Testament, 1592

The Earl of Southampton, painted by Nicholas Hilliard in about 1594

SERIOUS WRITING
Henry Wriothesley, the Earl of Southampton, was Shakespeare's patron. While the playhouses were shut, Shakespeare wrote two long poems, *Venus and Adonis* and *The Rape of Lucrece,* and dedicated them to his patron. This was Shakespeare's bid to be taken seriously as a writer. Playwrights were looked down on, but poets were respected, especially if they had aristocratic patrons.

Lavender

Sage

Marjoram

Rosemary

Cautery

Elizabethan golden pomander set with precious stones

Each section held a different herb

SMELLY CITY
Many Londoners tried to protect themselves from the plague by carrying pomanders (decorative containers holding sweet-smelling herbs). London was dirty and smelly, and all kinds of garbage was left to rot in the streets. People thought that there was a link between the plague and the bad air in the city.

BAD MEDICINE
Doctors during Shakespeare's time sometimes used a white-hot metal rod called a cautery to burst the swellings, called buboes, that appeared in the armpits and groins of plague victims. This treatment was extremely painful and did little to help the patient to recover.

A hat topped with ostrich feathers was the height of fashion

Clay pipes were introduced to England from the Americas in 1586

SCENTS FOR THE SENSITIVE

Nobody was more sensitive to the stench of London than the fashionable nobility. Rich women swung their jeweled pomanders in front of them as they walked. Gentlemen filled the air around them with tobacco smoke, hoping that it would protect them from the plague.

The skeletons in this engraving symbolize the plague

RUNNING AWAY

In 1592, everyone who was able to fled from London. Unfortunately, the plague followed them. Touring companies of actors may have helped to spread the plague. By 1593, the disease had struck other towns and cities in the country, including Shrewsbury, Nottingham, Lichfield, Derby, Leicester, and Lincoln.

The pomander hung on a chain around the woman's waist

STRANGE CURES

There were no effective treatments for the plague, but apothecaries, who were a cross between pharmacists and doctors, made up medicines to sell. They stored oils, herbs, and all kinds of other ingredients for their cures in pottery medicine jars. In *Romeo and Juliet*, Shakespeare describes an apothecary's shop, full of strange things, such as "skins of ill-shaped fishes" and "musty seeds."

A gallant (fashionable man) with a noblewoman

Enemies and protectors

THE POPULARITY OF THE theater in London attracted hostility from powerful enemies. The Lord Mayor and his aldermen saw any large gathering as a threat to law and order, and were always trying to close the playhouses down. Many city officials were also Puritans, who were against any form of entertainment. Fortunately, the actors had some powerful protectors. They were supported by Queen Elizabeth and her courtiers, who loved to watch plays. The Earl of Essex, the Lord Admiral, and the Lord Chamberlain became patrons of acting companies, which were then named after them.

POWERFUL PATRONS
In 1594, the Lord Chamberlain, Henry Carey (1524–1596), became the patron of Shakespeare's theater company. Carey was the queen's cousin and one of her closest advisors. Being the patron of an acting company was a sign of status and power.

WHIPPED OUT OF TOWN
It was against the law to perform plays without the permission of a powerful noble, and the law said that players caught performing illegally were to be treated as "rogues, vagabonds, and sturdy beggars." They were whipped out of town and branded by being burned through the ear with a hot iron.

Members of the public were used to seeing criminals being punished in the streets

A beggar is whipped out of town

Lord Mayor

Aldermen, members of the council

Puritans dressed more simply than other people

Portrait of Ben Jonson (1572–1637)

SCANDALOUS!
In 1597, Ben Jonson was put in prison for writing *The Isle of Dogs*, a play said to be "full of scandalous matter." This shows that, despite their noble protectors, acting companies and playwrights could still get into trouble if they put on controversial plays. Jonson's play was banned and never published, so we do not know why the government found it so shocking.

POWERLESS PROTEST
The Lord Mayor and his council of aldermen were responsible for law and order in the city of London. The Lord Mayor had no control at all, however, over what went on outside the city walls, where most of the playhouses were built. All that he could do was to send letters to the queen's ministers, the Privy Council, complaining about the dangers of the theater.

ALL WORK AND NO PLAY
Puritans thought that people should spend all of their time in work or prayer. Playhouses, which stopped people from doing both, were under constant attack from Puritan preachers.

Some gentlemen were so busy applauding the players on stage that they did not notice they were being robbed

LESSONS IN LIFTING
London was full of thieves called cutpurses, many of whom worked in well-organized gangs. In 1585, a school for boy cutpurses was discovered in a London ale house at Billingsgate. The school was run by an ex-merchant called Mr. Wotton, who taught boys to steal by getting them to lift coins from a purse with bells attached to it. Boys had to learn to take the coins without ringing the bells.

Cutting a purse was called "nipping a bung" in criminal slang

The cutpurse waits for the right moment to cut the purse strings

A gentleman's well-cut clothes stood out in the yard, where the poorest members of the audience gathered, and were likely to attract the attention of a cutpurse

Pants were worn tucked inside boots for riding

COUNTRY GENTLEMAN
Many gentlemen rode up to London from the countryside on business and called at the playhouses for some entertainment. Visitors from outside London were less aware than city people of the risk of being robbed by a cutpurse. Robberies took place regularly in the playhouses. This provided the Lord Mayor with an argument for closing them, although he exaggerated the number of crimes committed. In 1597, he wrote to the Privy Council, to warn it that playhouses were meeting places for "thieves, horse stealers, and plotters of treason."

Boys made good cutpurses because they were small enough not to be noticed and had nimble fingers

ROBBING PLACE
Cutpurses got their name because they would cut the strings that tied a purse to its owner's belt. Playhouses were ideal places for the cutpurses to work because they were so crowded and everyone there was concentrating on the stage. Despite this, cutpurses were sometimes caught in the act and beaten up by angry members of the audience.

JIGS AND JOKES
Will Kemp
(c. 1560–1603)
was a founding
member and
also a sharer
in the Lord
Chamberlain's
Men. He was a
popular comic actor, and
always danced a jig at the
end of a play. Kemp had
amazing energy, and, in 1600,
he danced from London to
Norwich, a distance of more
than 100 miles (160 km).
It took him nine days.

The Lord Chamberlain's Men

WHEN THE LONDON playhouses reopened in 1594, after
their long closure due to the plague, Shakespeare joined a new
company called the Lord Chamberlain's Men. He wrote about
two plays a year for them and also worked as an actor.
The company performed at the Theatre in north London,
which was owned by James Burbage. His son Richard
was the star actor, and Cuthbert, another of his sons,
managed the business. Shakespeare was one of several
"sharers" who invested money in the company to pay
for costumes, playbooks, and the wages of actors and
stage hands. In return, they took a share of the profits.

SLY SWORDSMAN
William Sly (died 1608)
was, like Shakespeare,
a player and sharer in
the Lord Chamberlain's
Men. He was a skilled
swordsman, and often
played the roles of
fashionable gallants or
fiery young men like
Hotspur in *Henry IV
Part One* and Tybalt
in *Romeo and Juliet*.

*Many costumes
were made from
scratch by members
of the company*

*The stage
hand sweeps
up after a
show at the
Theatre*

HIRED HELP
Among the company's hired men were several
stage hands. Their job was to raise the playhouse
flag, make sure that props were in the right place,
fire the cannon, and clear up trash left behind by
the audience. They were also responsible for
operating special-effect devices, such as the crane
used to lower actors playing angels or gods from
the "heavens" above the stage.

*Costumes
and props
were kept
in baskets
when not
in use*

RICHARD'S RIVAL
Edward Alleyn (1566–1626) was the star of the Lord Admiral's Men, and Richard Burbage's only real rival. He made his name playing Marlowe's heroes Dr. Faustus and Tamburlaine. Thomas Nashe wrote that no tragic actor in history "could ever perform more in action than famous Ned Allen."

TRAGIC TRANSFORMATION
Shakespeare wrote his greatest tragic roles for Richard Burbage (1568–1619). Burbage was famous for transforming himself into characters. Writer Richard Flecknoe said Burbage would "take off himself with his clothes," and "never assumed himself again until the play was done."

Dress, to be worn by a boy player playing a woman

Tireman admiring a new wig

COSTUME CARE
The tireman was in charge of his company's most valuable property – the costumes. Some of the costumes were bought from London tailors, and some were made by the company. Others were donated or sold to the players by courtiers, who did not like to be seen wearing the same outfit more than once.

Work table, where costumes were made and altered to suit new roles

BEHIND THE SCENES
At the modern Globe theater in London, England, a room has been set up to show visitors what a tiring, or dressing, room would have looked like in Shakespeare's day. Costumes, wigs, and props were stored in the tiring room, and it was also the place where some of the costumes would have been made. Between scenes, the players made their hurried costume changes here.

Building the Globe

In 1597, THE THEATRE was forced to close. It had been built on rented land, and the Burbages' agreement with the landowner had come to an end. The landowner refused to renew the lease because he hoped to keep the playhouse for himself and reuse its valuable oak timbers. Desperate to find a home for their players, the brothers came up with a plan. During the Christmas holidays of 1598, they hired workmen to pull the Theatre down. They took the oak timbers by boat across the river to Bankside, where they used them to build a new playhouse. They decided to call it the Globe.

The Globe's stage, as imagined by George Cruikshank in 1863, with Victorian-style scenery and curtains

Round pegs and joints

Square pegs and joints

KNOCK DOWN
The wooden joints of the Theatre were attached with pegs, which meant that the Burbages and their helpers could knock them apart using hammers. The undamaged timbers were then reassembled on the new site to make the frame of the Globe.

WALL STORY
After making the frame, the builders installed wall panels. Timber-framed buildings sometimes had walls made from wattle (woven mats of hazel stems) covered with daub (a mixture of clay, lime, straw, horsehair, and dung). Walls were also made using thin strips of wood called lath, plastered with lime, horsehair, and sand.

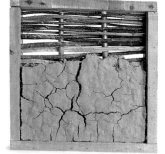

SOMETHING OLD, SOMETHING NEW
Inside the Globe, skilled carpenters used special tools to carve, drill, and chisel decorative features. The interior was colorful, with the stage columns painted to look like marble. The Burbages made sure that their new playhouse was an improvement on the old one.

Auger for boring holes in wood

Awls for making small holes

Billhook for pruning and lopping

Hammer

Broad ax

Hand saw

Chisel

Gentlemen's room for wealthy audience members

Gallery seats

Hell (space beneath the stage)

THE WOODEN O

This model gives us an idea of how the "Wooden O," as Shakespeare called his playhouse, may have looked. It is based on a 1596 sketch of the Swan playhouse, and on descriptions by visitors to the original building. Excavations in 1989 revealed that the Globe was 99 feet (30 m) wide.

Stamp showing the Globe with eight sides (it actually had 20 sides)

Pole for the playhouse flag

Upper rooms, where cannons were fired as a sound effect

The Rose

The Swan

The Globe

FLYING THE FLAG

Each playhouse had its own flag, flown on days when a play was being performed. The flags could be seen across the river in the city, where most of the potential audience lived. The Globe also had a sign above its entrance, depicting Hercules carrying a globe.

TO TILE OR NOT TO TILE?

Most new buildings in London in 1598 had tiled roofs, but the Burbages decided to use layers of straw or reeds called thatch for the roof of the Globe theater. Thatched roofs were far cheaper than tiles, but they were also much more of a fire risk.

Thatched roof shielded the galleries from the weather

In a play, the balcony could represent castle battlements or an upper window

Heavens (stage roof) – the underside was painted to look like a starry sky

Two columns held up the heavens

Stage stuck out into the yard, where the poorest people stood to watch the plays

35

Staging a play

Morion, a type of Spanish helmet

PLAYS AT THE GLOBE theater were performed in the afternoons, by daylight. There was only a limited amount of scenery, but there were some wonderful special effects. Angels and gods were lowered from the "heavens," and devils and ghosts came up through a trapdoor in the stage. Philip Henslowe, the owner of the Rose playhouse, had "a frame for the heading" for pretending to behead a man on stage. At the back of the stage, there was a curtained-off area used for displaying "discoveries" – picture-like scenes, such as characters lying dead or asleep. There was no director in charge of a production. The players knew what was expected of them, and they worked out the staging together.

Rapier was used for fencing

Dagger was used in the left hand

Rapier was kept in a scabbard that hung from the belt

SWAN STAGE
In 1596, a Dutch visitor named Johannes de Witt sketched the Swan playhouse, giving us the only image from that time of a Shakespearean stage. It is bare apart from a bench. The scene might be set anywhere, from a palace to the deck of a ship.

PLAYING SOLDIERS
When players rushed on stage in full armor, waving swords, the audience knew that they were watching a battle. If the players carried scaling ladders, as in *Henry V*, the battle became a siege. In all their battle scenes, even those set in ancient Rome, the players used the latest weapons and armor.

PLAY PLOT
The "platt," or plot, of a play was stuck on a board and hung on a peg backstage. It listed the scenes, with the exits and entrances of all the characters. During a performance, the players needed to refer to the platt because they had not read the whole play. Each player was given only his own part to learn. This is the platt for *The Seven Deadly Sins, Part Two*, performed at the Theatre from 1590 to 1591.

CONVINCING DISPLAY
A "beheaded man" could be shown on stage using two actors and a special table. This illusion would be set up in the "discovery space" at the back of the stage. Hidden hands would pull back the curtains, revealing to the audience what looked like the body of a man, with his head cut off and displayed at his feet.

SPILLED BLOOD
Pigs' or sheeps' blood was sometimes used to add gory realism to scenes of violent death. In one play, *The Rebellion of Naples*, a character had a fake head cut off. The head contained a pig's bladder, filled with blood, which gushed all over the stage.

"Our statues and our images of gods ...
Our giants, monsters, furies,
beasts and bugbears,
Our helmets, shields, and
vizors, hairs and beards,
Our pasteboard marchpanes
and our wooden pies ..."

RICHARD BROME
List of playhouse properties in *The Antipodes*

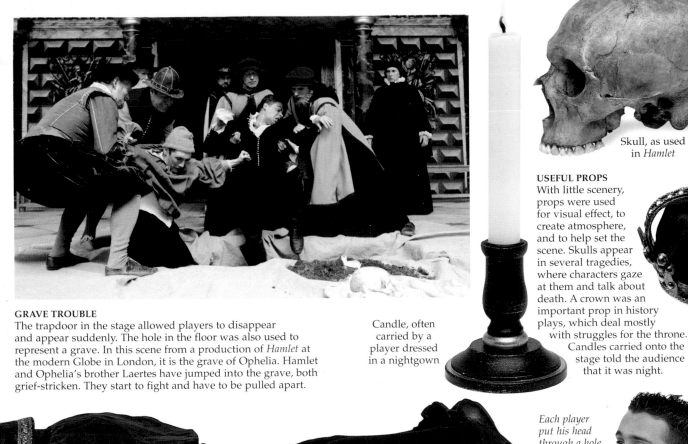

GRAVE TROUBLE

The trapdoor in the stage allowed players to disappear and appear suddenly. The hole in the floor was also used to represent a grave. In this scene from a production of *Hamlet* at the modern Globe in London, it is the grave of Ophelia. Hamlet and Ophelia's brother Laertes have jumped into the grave, both grief-stricken. They start to fight and have to be pulled apart.

Skull, as used in *Hamlet*

USEFUL PROPS

With little scenery, props were used for visual effect, to create atmosphere, and to help set the scene. Skulls appear in several tragedies, where characters gaze at them and talk about death. A crown was an important prop in history plays, which deal mostly with struggles for the throne. Candles carried onto the stage told the audience that it was night.

Royal crown

Candle, often carried by a player dressed in a nightgown

Each player put his head through a hole in the table

Ruff was placed around the player's neck after he had put his head through the hole in the table

The table surrounded by a curtain to hide what is underneath

The actor had to be careful not to blink or move

Music and dance

FROM THE ROYAL COURT to the peasant's cottage, music could be heard everywhere in Shakespeare's England. Many people played instruments, and, according to the 1588 book *In Praise of Music*, workers of all kinds kept up "a chanting and singing in their shops." When people went to see a play, they expected to hear good music. In Shakespeare's plays, there are more than 300 stage directions calling for music. He used it to create atmosphere, just as it is used in films today. Trumpets and drums, for example, were played in battle scenes. Shakespeare also wrote more than 70 songs for his characters to sing.

A boy plays a viol to accompany a lively dance, late 1500s

ROYAL GIFT
This instrument was invented in 1580 by London instrument maker John Rose. He named it after Orpheus, a mythical ancient Greek musician. Rose is thought to have presented this, his first orpharian, to Queen Elizabeth I, who was an avid and skilled musician.

Wire strings

Elaborately carved walnut body, inset with pearls and rubies

16th-century orpharian

A SPRING IN YOUR STEP
Many different dances were popular in Shakespeare's day. The galliard was a lively court dance with springing steps, leaps, and kicks, while the pavane was a stately dance, performed by a row of couples. Using long, gliding steps, ladies and gentlemen advanced, retreated, bowed, and curtsied. Away from court, people enjoyed less formal dances, such as the wild morris, danced with jangling bells strapped to the legs.

Triangle   *Lute*

Couple dancing the galliard, by Flemish artist Hieronymus Francken the Elder, 1540–1610

Serenade in front of Silvia's window, by John Gilbert, c. 1860

LOVE SONG
In Two Gentlemen of Verona, Thurio, who is in love with Silvia, hires musicians to "give some evening music to her ear." They perform one of Shakespeare's many love songs, "Who is Silvia?" A piece of music performed beneath a woman's window in an attempt to win her love is known as a serenade.

SOUNDS FOR CLOWNS
The pipe and tabor were played at the same time by one person. The musician beat the tabor (drum) with one hand, while playing notes on the pipe with the other. The pipe and tabor were used to accompany jigs – the clowns' dances that were traditionally featured at the end of shows and plays.

Pipe

MYSTERIOUS MELODIES

The hautboy, or shawm, made an eerie, solemn sound, which Shakespeare used to create an atmosphere of dread in his tragedies. Hautboys were often played before ghosts appeared on the stage.

This was a woodwind instrument like an oboe

Pipes produced a single continuous note called a drone

Hautboy

16th-century engraving by Crispin de Passe

LOVERS' LUTES

Lutes were often played by men when they were wooing women (trying to win their love). In *The Taming of the Shrew*, Petruchio tries to give hot-tempered Katherina a lute lesson. It ends with her smashing Petruchio over the head with his lute!

DANCE MUSIC

The viol was played with a bow, like a violin or viola. It was used mainly to accompany dances. In *Twelfth Night*, the foolish Sir Andrew Aguecheek "plays o' the viol-de-gamboys" in order to appear fashionable.

Second drone pipe

Musician blew air through mouthpiece

Viol made in the 1600s

BAGPIPE BLUES

In Shakespeare's time, the bagpipe was a popular instrument in England. It was played mostly in the open air for country dances. Falstaff, in *Henry IV Part One*, says that he feels as melancholy as "the drone of a Lincolnshire bagpipe."

Bag was made of leather

The tune was played with the fingers on this pipe

Bagpipe

Classic lute

"Let the sounds of music creep in our ears"

WILLIAM SHAKESPEARE
Lorenzo in *The Merchant of Venice*

The sheep's gut strings were plucked with the fingers and thumb

SOOTHING SOUNDS

The lute was a stringed instrument that was plucked to produce light and delicate notes. Many people in Shakespeare's day believed that its sweet, soothing sound had the ability to heal. In *King Lear*, the mad king is brought to his senses with music – almost certainly played on a lute.

Clothes and costumes

PLAYERS IN SHAKESPEARE'S day always dressed in clothes of their own time. The late 1500s was a wonderful time for fashion. Noblemen and women paraded around like peacocks in spectacular outfits that were padded to create startling shapes and slashed to display extra colors and fabrics. There were strict laws about clothes, which were worn as a sign of rank. Nobody below the rank of baron could wear cloth of silver, and people caught dressing above their station could be arrested and locked in the stocks. Players were the only people who were allowed to break these laws, by dressing as nobles on stage.

Leather and satin gloves

SWEET GLOVES
Fashionable ladies wore gloves scented with perfumes, such as musk and ambergris. In *Much Ado About Nothing*, Hero says, "These gloves the Count sent me; they are an excellent perfume."

17th-century diamond and amethyst necklace

COVERED IN JEWELS
Ladies covered themselves with glittering items of jewelry, including necklaces, rings, and earrings. They also wore diamonds and pearls sewn into their dresses, ruffs, hair, and shoes. The boy players wore cheaper costume jewelry made from glass because ladies would not have given away their valuable jewels.

Ruff made from lace

ALL PUFFED UP
Wealthy women in the late-16th century wore wide dresses with huge, padded sleeves. As a rule, the less practical the outfit, the higher the rank of its wearer. This dress is so impractical that its wearer would have had to go through doors sideways!

Elizabeth Buxton by Robert Peake, c. 1589

Sleeves stuffed with bombast, or horsehair

Skirt held out by a farthingale frame

FASHIONS FOR THE STAGE
Modern productions of Shakespeare's plays use clothes from many different periods of history. These 1920s designs for a production of *As You Like It* are early-1500s in style. Other productions of the play have been set in Victorian, Elizabethan, or modern times. In Shakespeare's day, the players often dressed extravagantly, which is one reason why people flocked to the playhouses. It wasn't important whether costumes were historically accurate because few people were aware of how fashions had changed throughout history.

ELIZABETHAN EXAGGERATION

Under Queen Elizabeth, the clothes worn by gallants grew more exaggerated. Ruffs, which first appeared in the 1560s, grew larger and larger, while hips and shoulders were padded to make the waist look narrow. Leg coverings often came in three sections – the round trunk hose at the top; the canions going to just below the knee; and the nether stockings worn underneath. The aim was to wear as many different fabrics and colors as possible.

Linen ruff stiffened with starch

A cartwheel ruff framed the face, making it look as if it were on a plate

Boy's hat

Gallant's hat

HATS OFF!

Men wore hats most of the time. Many gallants wore hats decorated with ostrich feathers, which they swept in front of them while bowing, as a greeting. In *Hamlet*, a gallant called Osric keeps waving his hat about. Hamlet says to him, "Put your bonnet to the right use; 'tis for the head."

Doublet with padded "peascod" belly

Trunk hose

Every gallant carried a sword

Canions

Nether stockings

A gallant of the 1580s, when ruffs were at their largest

A gallant of the 1590s, when smaller ruffs were back in fashion

FUNCTIONAL FASHION

Less wealthy men wore more practical versions of the clothes worn by gallants. They used cheaper fabrics such as wool instead of velvet or silk, and might have worn plain knee breeches rather than trunk hose and canions. They wore a ruff but did not worry if it was not the fashionable size.

THE RIGHT SHOES

This carved horn was used by a gallant in the 1590s to help him slip on his shoes. It is engraved with the image of a man of fashion. To a gallant, the right footwear was as important as the right ruff or doublet.

41

The boy player

ONLY MEN COULD ACT ON THE English stage in Shakespeare's time, so women's roles were performed by boys. Although these actors were called boy players, they probably played females until they were in their 20s. Shakespeare sometimes had fun by making the boy players act the parts of women disguised as men. Rosalind, the heroine of *As You Like It*, pretends to be a man called Ganymede. In disguise as Ganymede, Rosalind, who is in love with Orlando, offers to help him practice his wooing techniques by pretending to be the object of his affections – herself. So the boy playing Rosalind had to act as a woman, pretending to be a man, playing at being a woman!

A WOMAN AS A WOMAN!
In the film *Shakespeare in Love*, Gwyneth Paltrow plays a woman who disguises herself as a boy because she wants to act. After watching her play Juliet in *Romeo and Juliet*, an outraged royal official leaps onto the stage shouting "That woman is a woman!"

The tireman lowers the skirt over the farthingale

Pulling the laces tight will give the boy a waist

4 SKIRT OVER HOOP
The tireman helps the boy into a beautiful, embroidered skirt, which will show through a gap at the front of the dress.

Wheel, or French, farthingale

3 OUTSTANDING!
The boy steps into a hooped farthingale, which the tireman will fasten around his waist to make the skirt of the dress stand out.

2 HELPING HANDS
Next, the boy player puts on a tight upper garment called a bodice. He needs some help from the tireman, who laces up the back.

FASHIONABLE FIGURES
The women's fashion at the time for exaggerated hips and rear ends was achieved with a farthingale – a series of hoops made of whalebone, wood, or wire – or a padded belt called a bum roll. This fashion was a great help to boy players trying to look convincingly female.

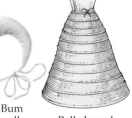

Bum roll

Bell-shaped farthingale

Wheel farthingale

The petticoat protects the skin from the stiff fabric of the rest of the costume

1 FIRST THINGS FIRST
In the tiring room of the playhouse, a boy player is getting ready to go on stage. He is playing Rosalind, the heroine of *As You Like It*. He begins his transformation by putting on a petticoat.

The real thing

A boy player needed the help of the company's tireman to get ready for his performance. To play the part of a noblewoman, he would dress in clothes that might once have been worn by a real noblewoman. Once a boy was wearing his farthingale, dress, makeup, and wig, the audience found him convincing as a female. English travelers to other European countries were amazed to see real women acting there.

"If I were a woman I would kiss as many of you as had beards that pleased me."

WILLIAM SHAKESPEARE
Rosalind in *As You Like It*

Mortar
and pestle

Lead

Tin

Talc

Green fig

PASTY PASTES
There were various recipes for white face makeup, or ceruse. One was a mixture of talc and tin, which was burned in a furnace for three days. The ash was then ground up with green figs and vinegar using a mortar and pestle. Another recipe used poisonous lead as an ingredient.

English roses

Pale skin was seen as a sign of nobility, because people with tanned skin were likely to be manual workers who spent most of their time in the sun. Another sign of beauty was a pair of blushing, rosy cheeks. Boy players used the same kind of makeup as noblewomen when they were acting the parts of court ladies.

A SPLASH OF COLOR
Red blusher was made by grinding a mineral called cinnabar or by crushing the roots of the madder plant. The red pigment, known as vermilion or fucus, was used to add color to the cheeks and the lips.

Cinnabar

Padded sleeves

Flat, stiff front called a stomacher

A fluttering fan made a good prop for a boy playing a woman

Rosalind's dress is one of the most expensive costumes in the tiring house

Luxurious beaded satin fabric

5 WALK LIKE A WOMAN
The dress is fitted over everything to complete the outfit, and the boy steps into a pair of high-heeled shoes. These will be hidden by the long dress, but wearing them will help him to walk on the stage in a stately and ladylike manner.

6 MISTRESS OF MIRTH
After putting on makeup, a small ruff, and a wig, the boy player's transformation into a woman is complete. He is ready to step out on to the playhouse stage as Rosalind. He repeats his first line to himself: "Dear Celia, I show more mirth than I am mistress of," and nervously flicks his fan.

The audience

PLAYGOING BECAME THE most popular form of entertainment for Londoners in the late-16th century. As many as 3,000 people would gather to watch any one performance. Playhouses drew their audiences from all walks of life. Farmers, seamstresses, soldiers, sailors, apprentices, and servants stood side by side in the crowded yard. Foreign tourists, lawyers, and merchants filled the gallery seats, and wealthy nobles sat in the gentlemen's rooms next to the stage, so that they could show off their expensive clothes.

IN THE GALLERY
In this early 1900s drawing of the Globe, fashionable audience members are watching a performance of *Henry IV* from the lowest gallery.

The apple wives found it hard to make a living if the playhouses were closed

SHAKESPEARIAN SNACKS
Apples and pears were for sale as snacks in the playhouses in Shakespeare's time. Different varieties were available at different times. The first apples to ripen were called "Juneaters" because they were ready for eating on June 29 – St. John's Day. Another variety was called the John apple because it kept well and could be stored until the following St. John's Day.

Williams pears

Pippins, grown in orchards in Kent, were the most common variety of apple

Pippin apples

Apples were bought as gifts for noblewomen

CARPET OF NUTS
In 1988 and 1989, archaeologists found that the yards of the Rose and Globe had been covered with hazelnut shells. The shells had been mixed with ash and used as a floor covering to keep the yards dry in wet weather. Some may have been dropped by the audience, because nuts were a popular snack.

BUSINESS AND PLEASURE
Female fruit sellers called apple wives loved the large audiences they found at playhouses like the Globe. The apple wives wandered around the yard and the galleries carrying baskets of apples and pears. They had no trouble finding hungry customers to buy their fruit, and they could enjoy the play as they worked.

According to the accounts of some theatergoers, groundlings stank of garlic and onions

Garlic cloves

The groundlings often heckled the players, shouting vulgar comments and throwing apples if they got bored

Money was carried in a purse dangling from a belt because few clothes at the time had pockets

Tankards were usually made from either pewter or wood

SHABBY SCARECROWS
The people who stood in the yard were called "groundlings" by the richer members of the audience. They were also nicknamed "scarecrows" because of their shabby appearance, or "stinkards" because of the way they smelled. They were sweaty and dirty, and people complained about their smelly breath.

THEATER THIEVES
Playgoers risked being robbed by a cutpurse. Stealing from groundlings in the crowded yard was easiest. But some thieves dressed as gentlemen to avoid attracting attention and worked in the galleries, where the richest pickings were to be found.

GETTING MERRY
Groundlings guzzled ale from tankards, like the one above, but the gallery crowd preferred wine. In several plays, Shakespeare's characters drink a strong Spanish wine called sack. In *The Merry Wives of Windsor*, Sir John Falstaff says that if he had a thousand sons he would teach them all to "addict themselves to sack."

Crowds of stinkards would sometimes start fights and riots – even the actors on the stage were not safe when they went on the rampage

"Your stinkard has the self-same liberty to be there in his tobacco fumes which your sweet courtier hath."

THOMAS DEKKER
The Gull's Hornbook, 1609

COMFORT COSTS
It cost one penny to stand in the yard to watch a play. For an extra penny, playgoers could sit in one of the gallery seats. A cushioned seat in the gentlemen's rooms cost three pennies.

Coin found at the Rose playhouse

Shakespeare's comedies

Shylock

Portia

In Shakespeare's time, a comedy simply meant a light-hearted play with a happy ending. In the 1590s, Shakespeare wrote 10 comedies, most of them with plots taken from old love stories. He liked stories in which young lovers overcome various obstacles, such as disapproving parents or comical misunderstandings, before they are allowed to marry. The lovers might have to go on a journey, put on a disguise, or run away from home into the woods. But everything always turns out all right in the end. *Two Gentlemen of Verona*, for example, ends in preparations for a double wedding. Valentine says to his friend Proteus, "Our day of marriage shall be yours; one feast, one house, one mutual happiness."

POUND OF FLESH
In *The Merchant of Venice*, Shylock, a moneylender, goes to court claiming that the merchant Antonio owes him a pound of flesh for failing to repay a debt. Portia, the heroine, disguises herself as a lawyer to defend Antonio. She argues that Shylock is entitled to Antonio's flesh, but not to one drop of blood.

"FOOL I' THE FOREST"
The heroine of *As You Like It* is Rosalind, one of many characters who are banished from court and go to live in the Forest of Arden. Another is Jaques, a melancholy lord who hates society and life in our "miserable world." But he enjoys talking to Rosalind's jester, Touchstone, who shares his upside-down view of the world.

Jaques   Touchstone

LOVE AND MARRIAGE
These portraits may have been mounted in a locket to celebrate the couple's marriage. Although people were fascinated by love stories, in real life they rarely married for love. The upper classes in particular usually married for money, or to improve their social rank.

When the locket is closed, the lovers are face to face, as if kissing

16th-century locket containing miniatures painted by Nicholas Hilliard

DITCHED
Falstaff, the old rascal from the history plays, reappears in *The Merry Wives of Windsor*. He sends love letters to two "merry wives," hoping to get hold of their money. The wives learn that he has sent the same letter to each of them and plot revenge. In one scene, Falstaff hides in a basket of dirty laundry and is then dumped in a muddy ditch.

VALENTINE'S DAY
Valentine, the hero of *Two Gentlemen of Verona*, is exiled from Milan because he loves the Duke's daughter. He is captured by outlaws in the woods, and they are so impressed by his gentlemanly behavior that they ask him to become their leader. The play ends with Valentine finding love and winning a pardon for his outlaw friends.

Malvolio is usually stern and cold, so when he smiles continuously at Olivia she thinks that he has gone crazy

MAGIC AND MISCHIEF
A Midsummer Night's Dream is set in an enchanted wood, home to Oberon and Titania, king and queen of the fairies. Angry with Titania, Oberon asks his servant Puck to drop a love potion in her eyes while she sleeps. It makes her fall in love with the first creature she sees on waking – Bottom, a humble weaver. For his own amusement, Puck has given Bottom the head of an ass.

Bottom with the head of an ass

Malvolio dreams of being made Count Malvolio

Oberon relents and cures Titania with the juice of a herb, thought to be wormwood

Wormwood (*Artemesia absinthium*)

MARY PICKFORD & DOUGLAS FAIRBANKS in ALL TALKING "TAMING OF THE SHREW" ALL LAUGHING
UNITED ARTISTS PICTURE

Malvolio's name means "bad will"

Malvolio's costume is usually made as farcical as possible for the scene with Olivia

MAKING A GOOD WIFE
This poster advertises the 1929 movie of *The Taming of the Shrew*, the least romantic of Shakespeare's comedies. Petruchio, the hero, decides to marry Katherina for money, not love. Katherina is "renowned in Padua for her scolding tongue." The play shows how Petruchio goes about "taming" Katherina, turning her into an obedient wife.

Petruchio

MAD FOR LOVE
Malvolio, in *Twelfth Night*, is the conceited steward of Olivia, a rich and beautiful countess. Practical jokers send him a letter, supposedly from Olivia. It says that she adores him and commands him to wear yellow stockings with cross garters, and to smile constantly in her presence. Malvolio follows the instructions and ends up being locked in a dark room as a madman.

Olivia has sworn to wear a veil for seven years, mourning her dead brother

Olivia

Malvolio, the central character of the comic subplot in *Twelfth Night*

"And each several chamber bless Through this palace with sweet peace; And the owner of it blessed Ever shall in safety rest."

WILLIAM SHAKESPEARE
Oberon in *A Midsummer Night's Dream*

47

The King's Men

QUEEN ELIZABETH DIED on March 24, 1603, and the crown passed to her closest male relative, James VI of Scotland. He was crowned James I of England on July 25, 1603, founding the Stuart dynasty. James found much about England unfamiliar. He disliked London and resented the power of the Puritan merchants. Supporting the theater was one way he tried to keep the Puritans in their place. He became the patron of Shakespeare's company, which was renamed the King's Men. The company was asked to perform at court more than 13 times a year, instead of the three times a year under Elizabeth. To please the king, Shakespeare wrote *Macbeth*, a tragedy with a Scottish setting.

Spear from Shakespeare's name

SHAKESPEARE'S ARMS
One sign of Shakespeare's growing success was that in 1596 he received a coat-of-arms, the badge of a gentleman. Later, when King James became patron of his company, Shakespeare was entitled to wear the uniform of the royal household.

JAMES I OF ENGLAND
James I (1566–1625) was the only son of Mary Queen of Scots. He was crowned soon after Elizabeth's death but was unable to enter London to show himself to his subjects until March 15, 1604. He was kept away by a terrible new outbreak of the plague, which killed 30,000 Londoners and closed the playhouses for months. One of the new king's first acts was to make peace with Spain.

ROYAL TOUCH
These gold "touchpieces" were given by James to people suffering from a disease called scrofula. A royal touch was supposed to cure the disease. Kings and queens had been touching the sick since the 11th century, but the practice increased under the Stuarts.

NOBLE FROG
In the early 1600s, it became fashionable for courtiers to carry purses designed to look like unusual objects or animals, such as a bunch of grapes, a pair of bellows, or this frog. Although frogs were linked with witchcraft in *Macbeth*, they were also a symbol of spring, when ponds become full of noisy frogs.

Macbeth cries, "Hence, horrible shadow!" when he sees Banquo's ghost

The ghost of Banquo makes a terrifying appearance at a feast

Crow

Toad

FAMILIAR SHAPES
Witches were thought to have evil spirit helpers, called familiars, which took the shape of animals such as black cats, toads, and crows. James was obsessed with the threat of witchcraft and wrote a book on it called *Daemonologie*. He warned his readers of "the fearful abounding at this time in this country of detestable slaves of the devil, the witches." In the 17th century, hundreds of innocent people were hanged for witchcraft.

Black cat

MURDER AND TREASON
In *Macbeth*, the witches predict that the hero will be king of Scotland, but that his friend Banquo will be the father of kings. Macbeth murders King Duncan to seize the crown, then murders Banquo. King James believed he could trace his own family back to the noble Banquo, so he would have been flattered by Shakespeare's choice of subject matter.

THE CURSE OF MACBETH

One of the "weird sisters" wore this costume in a recent production of *Macbeth*. The black magic in the play has led to a belief among superstitious actors that *Macbeth* is cursed. There are many stories of accidents during productions. According to the 17th-century writer John Aubrey, bad luck followed the play from its first performance, when the boy playing Lady Macbeth fell sick and died. Actors try to beat the curse by never mentioning the play's title, calling it "the Scottish play" instead.

Actors say it is bad luck to wear costumes from Macbeth in any other production

This costume was used in a Royal Shakespeare production of Macbeth

The dark colors of the costume reflect the description by Shakespeare of the ugly "midnight hags"

Dress made of torn strips of cotton

Achilles drags Hector's body behind his chariot

Hector's horrified parents watch from Troy

A PROBLEM OF STYLE

This ancient Roman lamp shows a scene from the Trojan war, the subject of Shakespeare's *Troilus and Cressida*, one of his three "problem plays." Critics use this term because they are unable to fit the plays into the usual categories of comedy or tragedy. *All's Well That Ends Well*, *Measure for Measure*, and *Troilus and Cressida* share many features of comedy, but they are also dark and gloomy in mood. *Troilus and Cressida* ends with the Trojan Hector, killed by Achilles, "at the murderer's horse's tail, in beastly sort, dragg'd through the shameful field."

The famous tragedies

IN THE 1590S, SHAKESPEARE wrote only a few tragedies, concentrating on comedies and history plays. He returned to the form in the early 1600s, when he wrote *Hamlet*, *King Lear*, *Othello*, and *Macbeth* – plays that provided his star Richard Burbage with his greatest roles. This group of tragedies contains Shakespeare's most famous poetry, such as Prince Hamlet's soliloquies on the meaning of life. There are also exciting action scenes, such as the fencing duel at the end of *Hamlet*. The prince does not know that his opponent Laertes has a poisoned sword and means to kill him.

Hamlet thrusts at Laertes's right shoulder, scoring a hit

Laertes tries to stab Hamlet, who deflects the blow

Laertes defends himself against Hamlet

Laertes catches Hamlet off guard and cuts him with his poisoned sword – it will be his death blow

Hamlet is the better swordsman

Hamlet thrusts at Laertes's thigh

FIT FOR FIGHTING
Players had to be skilled at sword fighting. Gentlemen learned fencing as part of their education and wore swords with their everyday dress. So, if they saw clumsy fighting in a play, they would boo the players off the stage. Fencing matches were also a popular entertainment. They were often put on as sporting events in the playhouses.

DEADLY DUEL
Hamlet believes that his duel with Laertes is a friendly contest. But the play's villain, Claudius, has persuaded Laertes to kill Hamlet. In the duel, Laertes and Hamlet are both wounded by the poisoned sword. The dying Laertes then confesses to Hamlet, who uses the sword to kill Claudius before he dies himself. At the play's end, the stage is covered with dead bodies.

STREET FIGHTING
Shakespeare wrote sword fights into several of his plays. In *Romeo and Juliet*, Romeo's friend Mercutio fights Juliet's cousin Tybalt in a street brawl.

OTHELLO

This poster advertising a production of *Othello* shows the Moor preparing to kill his sleeping wife Desdemona.

ROAST ME IN SULFUR!
The hero of *Othello* is a Moor (North African) married to Desdemona. Iago, the villain, secretly hates Othello and plots to destroy him. He makes Othello suspect that Desdemona is unfaithful. Driven insane by jealousy, Othello murders his innocent wife. Too late, he realizes that he has made a mistake. "Roast me in sulfur!" he cries. "Oh Desdemona! Desdemona dead!"

Iago

Othello

Iago is Shakespeare's greatest villain. He takes advantage of Othello's trusting nature. The Moor never suspects "honest Iago" as he calls him.

Fencers used a light, thin stabbing sword called a rapier

Hamlet gazes at his father's ghost, but his mother Gertrude cannot see the ghost, and thinks that her son is insane

MOST UNNATURAL MURDER
In the 1947 film of the play *Hamlet*, Laurence Olivier played the prince. This is the tragedy of a Danish prince, ordered by the ghost of his father to avenge his "foul and most unnatural murder." He must kill the murderer who is both his uncle and his stepfather.

FOOLISH FATHER
In the play *King Lear*, an old king foolishly divides his kingdom between two wicked daughters and rejects the daughter who loves him. Furious at his daughters' ingratitude, Lear takes to a storm-swept heath. He suffers madness, but eventually comes to understand how foolish he has been.

Hamlet is the most complex of Shakespeare's heroes

Polonius, Laertes's father, is accidentally killed by Hamlet, who mistakes him for the king.

"So shall you hear Of carnal, bloody, and unnatural acts, Of accidental judgments, casual slaughters."

WILLIAM SHAKESPEARE
Horatio in *Hamlet*

The Roman plays

In the early 1600s, both Shakespeare and Ben Jonson wrote tragedies set in ancient Rome. This subject was familiar to educated members of their audiences, thanks to the influence of Roman writers like Seneca. Setting plays in Rome allowed playwrights to raise political issues without risking offending the government. Ben Jonson's *Catiline* deals with a plot to overthrow the Roman state, but the real subject of the play was the 1605 Gunpowder Plot to kill King James. Jonson could not have gotten away with writing about this directly, so he set his play in the distant world of ancient Rome.

Poster for a 1965 production of *Coriolanus*

OFFENDING PORTRAIT
Julius Caesar (100–44 BC) was the subject of Shakespeare's first play about Roman history. Caesar was an ambitious and successful Roman general and politician, who was eventually murdered because he started to act like a king. He was the first Roman to put his portrait on a coin, which offended many people. Previously, only dead Romans had been given this honor.

ROMAN REJECT
In his play *Coriolanus*, Shakespeare tells the story of an ambitious Roman nobleman called Coriolanus, who is a great warrior but a poor politician. He despises the ordinary people of Rome, but needs their support in order to be made consul, or head of state. When the people reject Coriolanus, he abandons Rome and joins the city's enemies, the Volscians.

Roman coin with the portrait of Julius Caesar

In the play Julius Caesar, *the ghost of the murdered leader returns to speak to Brutus, the man who killed him*

Brutus, who plans Caesar's murder

Mark Antony, who defeats Brutus in war

Brutus asks the ghost if he is "some devil that mak'st my blood turn cold and my hair to stare".

MURDERING HERO
The hero of Shakespeare's play *Julius Caesar* is not Caesar but his friend and killer Brutus. Brutus fears that Caesar wants to become king, and decides he must die so that Rome can remain free. However, the murder plunges the state into civil war. Mark Antony rouses the people of Rome against the killers with his famous speech, "Friends, Romans, countrymen, lend me your ears."

The folds of togas make good places for actors playing the killers in Julius Caesar *to hide their daggers*

Cobra, the type of snake with which Cleopatra may have killed herself

Cleopatra with her maid Charmian

LOVE BEFORE DUTY

Antony and Cleopatra is a sequel to *Julius Caesar*. Antony falls out with Caesar's heir, Octavius, when he falls in love with Cleopatra, the beautiful queen of Egypt. Lovestruck, Antony forgets his duties to Rome, and another civil war breaks out. The play ends with the suicide of the lovers. Antony stabs himself; and Cleopatra makes a deadly snake bite her.

1940s US actress Katherine Cornell as Cleopatra

TOGAS OR CLOAKS

Roman citizens dressed in elaborately folded robes called togas, which are now often worn in productions of Shakespeare's Roman plays. But Shakespeare would not have known what a toga was. He based his plays on Sir Thomas North's translations of the Greek writer Plutarch. North describes Romans wearing "mantles" and "cloaks," like courtiers did in Shakespeare's time.

SQUEAKING CLEOPATRA

Miss Darragh played Cleopatra to Jerrold Robertshaw's Antony in this early 20th-century production of Shakespeare's play. Cleopatra is Shakespeare's greatest female role. Witty, clever, and stronger than Antony, she dies imagining her story being performed on stage, with a boy playing her. She says, "I shall see some squeaking Cleopatra boy my greatness."

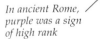

In ancient Rome, purple was a sign of high rank

Adventures and fairy tales

IN 1608, THE KING'S MEN TOOK over a second playhouse, at Blackfriars on the north side of the Thames River. Unlike the Globe, the new playhouse was an indoor theater, where plays were performed by candlelight. The Blackfriars was much smaller than the Globe, and entrance charges were higher. The new audience, made up of courtiers and other wealthy Londoners, inspired a new style of playwriting. Between 1608 and 1611, Shakespeare wrote four plays for the Blackfriars. Known as the romances, they have in common fairy-tale plots, the adventures of noble heroes and heroines, and families broken apart and reunited.

REGRET AND REUNION
This photograph from a 1966 production of *A Winter's Tale* shows Polixenes with King Leontes. The King imagines that Polixenes is having an affair with his wife and locks her away. The queen fakes her own death, filling Leontes with grief and regret, and the couple are ultimately reunited.

SHIPWRECK SPELL
The Tempest is about a magician called Prospero, the rightful Duke of Milan. He is overthrown by his brother and goes to live on an island with his daughter, his fairy helper Ariel, and a band of other spirits. He uses magic to cause a shipwreck that brings his enemies to the island for punishment.

Illustration for
The Tempest by
Robert Dudley, 1856

Prospero's spirits bring a banquet to the shipwrecked seafarers

NOVEL IDEA
Shakespeare found the basic ingredients for his romances in prose works like Sir Philip Sydney's *Arcadia* (1593). This long tale, a forerunner of the novel, follows the adventures of two disguised princes in their search for love.

ROMANTIC INFLUENCE
Shakespeare was also influenced by two playwrights, Francis Beaumont and John Fletcher, who had been writing stage romances since 1607. Fletcher later worked with Shakespeare on his last three plays, and took over from him as the main playwright for the King's Men.

Illustration for
Cymbeline by
Robert Dudley, 1856

*"... I come
To answer thy best
pleasure; be't to fly,
To swim, to dive
into the fire, to ride
On the curled clouds ..."*

WILLIAM SHAKESPEARE
Ariel in *The Tempest*

FULL OF SURPRISES
In the play *Cymbeline*, Posthumus and Imogen, the husband and wife hero and heroine, are forced to part when Posthumus is banished. The play follows their fortunes while they are apart. *Cymbeline* has more plot twists than any other Shakespearean play, with eight surprises in a row in the final scene.

Chest holding Thaisa, found on the seashore

MIRACULOUS MUSIC
Pericles is set in the Mediterranean, with shipwrecks and pirates featuring in the action. Pericles, Prince of Tyre, buries his wife Thaisa at sea after she dies giving birth to their daughter. Thaisa is washed ashore at Ephesus, where she is brought back to life by the miraculous healing power of music.

Illustration from *The Children's Shakespeare* by Charles Folkard, 1911

FANCY FASHION
A fashion for a type of court entertainment called a masque – a mixture of ballet, opera, and ornate costumes – influenced staging at the Blackfriars. At court, performers recited poems, sang, and danced in front of elaborate sets. The King and his courtiers often joined in. In *The Tempest*, Prospero stages his own masque with the help of magic.

The playwright's signature

Part of the legal document giving Shakespeare the rights to the house at Blackfriars

PERSONAL PROPERTY
In 1613, Shakespeare bought a house just around the corner from the Blackfriars playhouse. He may have intended to live there, or may simply have bought it as an investment. Shakespeare did not spend much time in his new house. He had already gone back to live in Stratford and would soon give up writing plays.

Woman in a masque costume, c. 1615

☼ ☾ Science and superstition

The sun and moon are important astrological signs

"It is the stars, the stars above that govern our conditions," says the Earl of Kent in *King Lear*. In Shakespeare's time, many people believed in astrology – the idea that heavenly bodies could control or influence life on Earth. Even Queen Elizabeth consulted an astrologer, the brilliant Dr. John Dee. And sailors used the sun and the stars to find their way at sea. Improvements in methods of navigation, such as the back-staff, meant that, by the 16th century, English ships were sailing into all of the world's oceans.

Protective leather case

Mirror made from obsidian, a glassy volcanic rock

MIRROR, MIRROR
Dr. John Dee (1527–1608) owned this "scrying mirror," which he said had been given to him by an angel. It was actually made by the Aztec people of Mexico, but no one knows how the doctor came to have it. Dee would gaze into the mirror, hoping to see spirits or visions of the future.

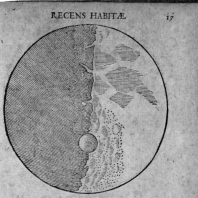

Galileo's 1610 book *The Starry Messenger*, showing the scientist's drawings of the cratered surface of the moon

Scale

The shadow vane was lined up so that its shadow fell on the horizon vane

The horizon vane was aimed at the horizon

STAR GAZING
In 1609, the Italian scientist Galileo Galilei (1564–1642) built a telescope and looked at the night sky through it. He published his discoveries in his book *The Starry Messenger*. Galileo was amazed to see thousands of stars, which no one had seen before. He also discovered four moons orbiting Jupiter, and studied craters and mountains on the surface of Earth's moon.

WELL-EQUIPPED

John Dee was an expert at navigating by the sun and stars, with the help of specialized equipment. This astronomical compendium incorporates an ingenious range of instruments to help guide the course of a ship, including a compass, a wind vane, and a sundial.

1625 engraving of an alchemist

THE SCIENCE OF THE STONE

Dee was also interested in alchemy, the scientific search for the magical "philosopher's stone," which could turn metals such as lead into gold. Ben Jonson made fun of this practice in his 1611 comedy *The Alchemist*. Jonson's alchemist, Subtle, is a fraud who cheats greedy and gullible people out of their money using lies and trickery.

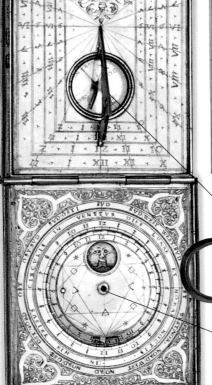

Sundial and compass

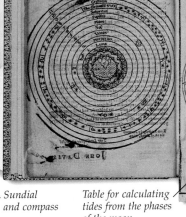

Table for calculating tides from the phases of the moon

Wind vane

Wind vane screws into place here

BEST BOOK

In 1595, scientist John Davis (c. 1550–1605) wrote *The Seaman's Secrets*, the most accurate guide to navigation of the 16th century. Davis was a skilled navigator and an experienced explorer. He made three voyages into the Arctic, hoping to find a route to China. Davis was eventually killed by pirates while on route to Sumatra, Indonesia.

A replica of Galileo's telescope

Galileo's telescope was a great improvement on a Dutch invention

The sighting vane was positioned at the estimated latitude

The navigator looked through the slit in the sighting vane

BACK TO THE SUN

John Davis invented the back-staff, an instrument for determining a ship's latitude, or north-south position, from the height of the sun. Earlier instruments, such as the cross-staff, forced navigators to stare into the sun. With a back-staff, navigators could turn their backs to the sun and use a shadow to measure its height.

Davis's back-staff was the most popular navigation instrument until well into the 17th century

SECRET STUDIES

John Gielgud starred as scientist-magician Prospero in the 1991 movie *Prospero's Books*, which was based on Shakespeare's *The Tempest*. Prospero is a mysterious character, who describes himself in the play as being "rapt in secret studies." Shakespeare created him at about the same time that Jonson was writing *The Alchemist*.

"These late eclipses of the sun and moon portend no good to us."

WILLIAM SHAKESPEARE
The Earl of Gloucester in *King Lear*

Return to Stratford

AFTER FINISHING WORK on *The Tempest* in 1611, Shakespeare returned to live in Stratford. Although he had inherited the house in Henley Street when his father died, he went to live in New Place, which he had bought for his family in 1597. William had become a wealthy man, and New Place was the second-largest house in the town. The playwright enjoyed only a few years of retirement. On April 23, 1616, he died, a month after completing his will. Shakespeare was buried at the Holy Trinity Church in Stratford, with the words "Curst be he that moves my bones" inscribed on his grave.

HOME STUDY
Shakespeare continued to write for about two years after his return to Stratford. He visited London from time to time to work with John Fletcher on the three plays *Henry VIII*, *Two Noble Kinsmen*, and a lost play called *Cardenio*. Shakespeare's fellow playwrights, including Ben Jonson, also visited him at New Place.

LAST LINES
In 1613, Shakespeare wrote his last lines for the theater in the play *Two Noble Kinsmen*. The scenes written by Shakespeare stand out because he used language in a more complicated way than Fletcher did. This little-known and rarely performed play tells the story of two friends, Palamon and Arcite. The characters, shown here in a production of the play at the modern Globe theater, both fall for the beautiful Emilia, and rivalry in love turns them into bitter enemies.

SOUND EFFECT BACKFIRES
On June 29, 1613, disaster struck at the Globe when the playhouse cannon was fired during a performance of *Henry VIII*. Sparks landed on the thatched roof and started a fire. The audience and the players all managed to escape from the fast-spreading flames, but the Globe was burned to the ground. At about this time, Shakespeare retired from writing and returned to Stratford for good. The loss of his old playhouse may have been the reason for his decision.

The cannon was fired to announce the arrival of the king, played by Richard Burbage

Elizabethan cannon with bronze barrel and reproduction wooden stand

The Globe was rebuilt on the foundations of the building destroyed by fire

RAISED FROM THE ASHES
The King's Men rebuilt the Globe at great expense and reopened it in 1614. They roofed it with fire-proof tiles instead of thatch. The company continued to perform there for the next 30 years.

HOME IS WHERE THE HEART IS
In 1607, Shakespeare's daughter Susanna went to live at Hall Croft in Stratford with her new husband John Hall. Shakespeare approved of the match and would have returned to Stratford for the wedding. During his last years working in London, Shakespeare returned to Stratford with increasing regularity. He probably attended most family events, such as his mother's funeral in 1608, and his granddaughter Elizabeth's christening in the same year.

A GOOD LIKENESS
In 1623, a stone monument to William Shakespeare was installed in the Holy Trinity Church. The painted statue is likely to be an accurate portrait of the playwright because it was approved by his family. The sculptor, Geerart Janssen, had a workshop near the Globe, and may have known Shakespeare himself.

IVDICIO PYLIVM GENIO SOCRATEM ARTE MARONEM,
TERRA TEGIT, POPVLVS MÆRET, OLYMPVS HABET

STAY PASSENGER, WHY GOEST THOV BY SO FAST,
READ IF THOV CANST, WHOM ENVIOVS DEATH HATH PLAST
WITH IN THIS MONVMENT SHAKSPEARE: WITH WHOME,
QVICK NATVRE DIDE WHOSE NAME, DOTH DECK Y TOMBE,
FAR MORE, THEN COST: SIEH ALL, Y HE HATH WRITT,
LEAVES LIVING ART, BVT PAGE, TO SERVE HIS WITT.
OBIT ANO DO 1616
ÆTATIS 53 DIE 23 AP.

WILL'S WILL
In his will, Shakespeare left his lands and houses in Stratford and London to his eldest daughter Susanna. His younger daughter Judith received £300, a large sum at the time. Shakespeare's wife Anne received only his second-best bed, but it is likely that she continued to live at New Place until she died in 1623.

Mourning jewelry was often decorated with reminders of death such as skulls and skeletons

17th-century mourning ring

REMEMBER ME
Shakespeare also left money to his closest friends from the King's Men – Richard Burbage, Henry Condell, and John Heminges – so that they could buy gold mourning rings. The playwright hoped that wearing the rings after his death would help them to remember him.

Pearls surround the skull and crossbones at the center of this pendant

Book publishing

17th-century image of a compositor laying out letters for printing

By THE TIME Shakespeare was writing, all kinds of books were being mass-produced in print shops all over Europe; but he had little interest in seeing his plays in print. They were written to be performed and could reach a far larger audience at the Globe than they would as books. Shakespeare's plays belonged to his company, and about half of them were published during his lifetime as little books called quartos. They were published when their performing days were over, or when the company needed to raise money. It was not until seven years after his death that some fellow actors published Shakespeare's plays in a single volume which is known as the First Folio.

HARD PRESSED
The printing process in Shakespeare's day was long and slow, and required the input of several people. A pressman called a compositor laid metal letters in a frame called a chase. This was placed on the "coffin," where a pressman inked the letters with a leather ball. Another pressman placed the paper on a frame called a tympan, and lowered it on to the coffin. He then slid the coffin under a printing plate called a platen, and pulled the bar to lower the platen, pressing the paper onto the inky letters.

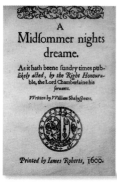

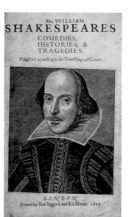

SIXPENNY QUARTO
This edition of *A Midsummer Night's Dream* was printed in 1600 by James Roberts, one of 21 printers in London at the time. Each copy was sold for six pennies – six times the cost of seeing the play on stage. The name quarto, meaning fourth, comes from the fact that four pages were printed at once, on each side of a single sheet. This was folded twice and cut to make eight pages of text.

FIRST FOLIO
In 1623, Henry Condell and John Heminges published 36 of Shakespeare's plays in the leather-bound First Folio. A folio, from the Latin word for leaf, is a large book with pages made up of standard sheets, or leaves, of paper folded in half. Hemminges and Condell wrote that their aim was "only to keep the memory of so worthy a friend, and fellow alive, as was our Shakespeare."

Heavy platen, or printing plate

Sturdy wooden frame

Hand press

The illustrations on these pages show six varieties of iris

Tympan

Embroidered carrying bag for pocket book

COLORING IN
Illustrations such as these beautiful flowers from John Gerard's *History of Plants* of 1597 were sometimes included in printed books. The 1,800 pictures in this book were printed in black and white from carved blocks of wood, and color was added by hand. The slow hand-coloring process made this an extremely expensive book.

Pressmen usually worked in pairs

Detail from a 17th-century engraving of a print shop

Bar to lower platen

BOOK IN A BAG
It was fashionable in Shakespeare's day to read while walking in the open air, and pretty, pocket-sized books were ideal for this. Pocket books often contained short religious texts, to appeal to Puritans, or almanacs, which were predictions of the coming year's events.

16th-century pocket book, with a gallant in a feathered hat for decoration

This book was designed to be kept on a shelf in a row with identically bound editions of other Shakespeare plays

Sliding coffin

Leather ink ball, stuffed with horsehair

Detail from a 17th-century engraving of a pressman lifting a printed sheet off the press

Shakespeare's coat of arms

UNLIMITED EDITIONS
By 1913, when this copy of *Romeo and Juliet* was printed, hundreds of editions of Shakespeare's plays had been published. This expensive volume, with its embossed leather cover, was designed to look impressive in the library of an upper-class house. Cheaper editions were also being read around the world by an audience far larger than Shakespeare ever could have imagined possible.

Shakespeare's legacy

"HE WAS NOT OF AN AGE, BUT FOR ALL TIME," wrote the playwright Ben Jonson to describe his friend William Shakespeare, and he has been proved right. Over the years, styles of acting and staging plays have changed many times, but Shakespeare has not gone out of fashion. His plays have been translated into almost every language and are still being performed all around the world. They have inspired ballets, operas, musicals, films, and paintings. Shakespeare's other great legacy is to the English language itself. Hundreds of everyday words and phrases appeared first in a Shakespeare play. These include "bare-faced," "cold-blooded," "excitement," and "fair play." We all regularly quote from Shakespeare without realizing it.

DREAMY DISH
Designed in 1853 by Irish sculptor W. B. Kirk, this porcelain fruit bowl is part of a Shakespeare dessert service. Each piece was decorated with a lively scene from *A Midsummer Night's Dream*.

Herbert Beerbohm Tree as Cardinal Wolsey in *Henry VIII*

CAPTURED IN GLASS
This stained-glass window depicting some of Shakespeare's comic characters is in Southwark Cathedral, London, where the playwright worshipped. The window was designed by Christopher Webb and was unveiled in 1954 on the anniversary of Shakespeare's death. Every year, on Shakespeare's birthday, a celebration of his life and works is held in the aisle beneath the window.

CARTOON CULTURE
In the 1990s, some of Shakespeare's plays were animated for children's television. In this scene from *A Midsummer Night's Dream*, the fairy king Oberon is pictured as he is about to awaken Titania from a spell. He touches her eyes with the magic herb, saying, "Now my Titania; wake you, my sweet queen."

SPECTACULAR SHAKESPEARE
British actor-manager Herbert Beerbohm Tree was famous for his spectacular productions of Shakespeare's plays in the late-19th and early-20th century. He used huge casts, lavish sets, and live animals. His dramatic style of acting was not to everyone's taste, but Shakespeare's characters can be played in many different ways.

Stratford's market square hung with banners for the Shakespeare Jubilee in 1769

STRATFORD CELEBRATIONS

Each year, millions of tourists from all over the world visit Stratford-upon-Avon to see where Shakespeare was born and raised. Tourists first came to Stratford in 1769, when actor and producer David Garrick organized the Shakespeare Jubilee. Although that festival was ruined by heavy rain, an annual Shakespeare Festival still takes place today.

PUTTING IT TO MUSIC

Shakespeare's plays have inspired several musicals and operas. In the 1940s and '50s, two plays were turned into popular musicals: *Kiss Me Kate*, a retelling of *The Taming of the Shrew*, and *West Side Story*, which is the tale of *Romeo and Juliet* set in the streets of New York. Operatic adaptations of Shakespeare's plays include Verdi's *Macbeth*, *Othello*, and *Falstaff*, all composed during the second half of the 19th century.

Howard Keel and Kathryn Grayson in the 1953 film *Kiss Me Kate*

Shakespeare's queen, Elizabeth, alongside two kings who feature in his plays, Henry V and Richard III

TEMPEST IN SPACE

The 1956 film *Forbidden Planet* took the story of *The Tempest* and set it in outer space. The magician Prospero became a scientist called Dr. Morbius, while his spirit helper Ariel was reborn as Robbie the Robot. Shakespeare's original shipwrecked seafarers became astronauts on a mission into space.

POETS' CORNER

In 1740, this statue of Shakespeare was set up in London's Westminster Abbey. It overlooks Poets' Corner, where some of Britain's greatest poets are buried or have memorials. Shakespeare is pointing to a scroll on which is written part of Prospero's speech from *The Tempest*: "Our revels now are ended."

WILLIAM SHAKESPEARE 1564 - 1616
BURIED AT STRATFORD-ON-AVON

Index

Acknowledgments

Dorling Kindersley would like to thank:
Models: Kate Adams, Annabel Blackledge, Ken Brown, Nick Carter, David Evans, John Evans, James Halliwell, Jamie Hamblin, James Parkin, Alan Plank, Dan Rodway, and Johnny Wasylkiw. **Makeup artists:** Jordana Cox, Hayley Spicer. **Props:** Ken Brown. **Wigs:** Darren and Ronnie at The Wig Room. **Armorer:** Alan M. Meek. **Stylist:** Judy Hill. **Costumes:** The RSC, Stratford. **Editorial assistance:** Carey Scott. **Index:** Lynn Bresler.

The publishers would like to thank the following for their kind permission to reproduce their photographs:
a=above; b=below; c=center; l=left; r=right; t=top

AKG London: 16tl, 20cl, 23br, 38bl, 39tr, 46bl, 51tl, 54cla, 54cl, 54br, 55cra, 57tl, 60tl, 61cl, 61bl, 63bc; British Library Add. 48027 Folio 650 11cr, Folio 57 Harley 1319 26cl; Erich Lessing 9clb, 38tl. Avoncroft Museum Historic Buildings: 34cl. Bridgeman Art Library: Beauchamp Collection, Devon 27br; Bristol City Museum and Art Gallery, UK 55c; British Library 25br, 30bc, 60c; Christie's Images 61br; Dulwich Picture Gallery, London, UK 32c; Dyson Perrins Museum, Worcester, UK 62tl; Fitzwilliam Museum, University of Cambridge 28cl; Guildhall Library, Corporation of London 20-21; Guildhall Library, Corporation of London, UK 55cl; Helmingham Hall, Suffolk, UK/Mark Fiennes 38cr; Linnean Society, London, UK 61tl; National Museums of Scotland 8b; Norfolk Museums Service (Norwich Castle Museum) UK 40br; Private Collection 11tl, 11bl, 28b, 30c, 36tl, 46cr, 54cr; Private Collection/Barbara Singer 27tl; Private Collection/Christie's Images 16tr; Private Collection/Ken Walsh 24-25; Private Collection/The Stapleton Collection: 23bl; Victoria & Albert Museum, London, UK 16r, 40bl; Walker Art Gallery Board of Trustees National Museums & Galleries on Merseyside 22c; Yale Center for British Art, Paul Mellon Fund, USA 34tr, 46br. British Library: 4bl, 18-19, 23tl, 61tr, 61cr. © The British Museum: 11(main image), 18tl, 19tr, 49br, 52c, 56ca; Chas Howson 21tr. Corbis: Robert Estall 16c. Photographic Survey Courtauld Institute of Art: Private Collection 30tl. By permission of the Trustees of Dulwich Picture Gallery: 33tc (detail). Dulwich College: 36cl. Museum of English Rural Life: 13tl. Mary Evans Picture Library: 8tl, 9cb, 12tl, 13br, 15tl, 15cr, 15bl, 17bl, 17bc, 19tl, 21bc, 22tl, 25tr, 29tr, 30clb, 30br, 32tl, 33tl, 48tl, 48tr, 48br, 54crr, 63t; Ames 56tr; Charles Folkard 55tl; ILN1910 44tl. Glasgow Museums; Art Gallery & Museums: 10tl, 11tr. Ronald Grant Archive: 47cr, 52tl, 52br, 53tc, 53br, 62cl, Prospero's Book © Allarts Enterprises 57br, Animated Tales of Shakespeare's A Midsummer Night's Dream © BBC 62c, The Winter's Tale 1966 © Cressida Film Productions 54tl, Forbidden Planet © MGM 63bl; Hamlet 1948 © Two Cities 51cl. Mary Rose Trust: 15tr, 27tc, 45cr. Museum of London Archaeology Service: Andy Chopping 45br. Courtesy of the Museum of London: 3, 10bl, 16bcl, 19bc, 22-23, 24br, 25tc, 34clb, 40cl, 48c, 50br. National Maritime Museum, London: 26-27, 56-57b, 57tc, 57tr, 58bc; Tina Chambers 20bcl. The Natural History Museum, London: 2bc, 37tr. Post Office Picture Library: Shakespeare's Theatre Postage Stamps © The Post Office 1995. Reproduced by kind permission of The Post Office. All rights Reserved 21tl, 21cl, 35tcl, 35tcr, 58br. Premier Brands: 26bl, 26br, 50tl, 50crb, 51tr, 51cr, 51bl, 51bll. Public Record Office: 59cl. Museum of the Royal Pharmaceutical Society: Jane Stockman 29cr. The Royal College of Music, London: Division viol by Barak Norman, London, 1692 39tl. St Bride Printing Library: 60-61. Science & Society Picture Library: 56bl. Science Museum: 48cl, 56-57c; John Lepine 28r. Shakespeare Birthplace Trust, Stratford-upon-Avon: 6cl, 6br, 6-7, 7bl, 7br; Malcolm Davies 10c, 60cl; By kind permission of Jarrold Publishing 6tl, 58tl, 59tl. Shakespeare's Globe: Donald Cooper 58cr; Nik Milner 32-33; John Tramper 37tl. Courtesy of the Trustees of the V&A Picture Library: 6bl, 40tl. Vin Mag Archive: SAC 42tl. The Wallace Collection: 26tl, 27tr. Warwick Castle: 36tr. Weald and Downland Open Air Museum: 7tr, 13c. Westminster Cathedral: 10cr. York Archaeology Trust: 24cl.

Jacket credits:
AKG London: back bl, back tr, front tr. Bridgeman Art Library: Christie's Images front tl; Private Collection front br; Private Collection/Barbara Singer back tlb. Corbis: front br. Mary Evans Picture Library: back bc, back tcl, front tcl; ILN 1910 front bl. National Maritime Museum, London: back cra. The Natural History Museum, London: front clb. Post Office Picture Library: back tcrr. Premier Brands: inside front br. Museum of the Royal Pharmaceutical Society: Jane Stockman back cla. Shakespeare Birthplace Trust, Stratford-upon-Avon: front cl; Malcolm Davies front cb. Courtesy of the Trustees of the V&A Picture Library: inside front cl. The Wallace Collection: inside front cr.

All other images © Dorling Kindersley.
For further information see:
www.dkimages.com